JN194969

**串揚げとふぐ料理の新世界**

# Kushinobo

Haruhiko Inui
乾　晴彦

旭屋出版

# Kushinobo and Fugu Cuisine Will Continue Evolving!

## 串揚げもふぐ料理も進化し続ける！

The year 2019 marks the 69th anniversary of fried skewers restaurant "Kushinobo", and 35th anniversary of fugu (blowfish) restaurant "Roppongi Hamato". *Kushinobo* and fugu belong to different categories in the food industry, however, both restaurants share the same concept of always pursuing to serve the best quality cuisine. They have become the fundamental wheels that run this company.

To depict our progress through the years, we have drastically renewed our previous "Kushinobo: The Delicious Deep-Fried Skewer Book" published in 2006 (reprinted to 4th edition) by introducing the unique menus that we serve at Kushinobo Special every year, as well as the fugu, truffles & caviar menus which we serve at "Roppongi Hamato".

I wish this book will surprise you with new and exquisite menu ideas along with the classic lineups, inspiring you to experience and explore the innovative world of *kushinobo* and fugu.

Kushinobo Co., Ltd. CEO **Haruhiko Inui**

2019 年で串揚げの『串の坊』は創業 69 年、天然とらふぐの『六本木　浜藤』は創業 35 年になります。串揚げと天然とらふぐという異業種の組み合わせですが、最高の食事を目指すという点でコンセプトは同じくし、会社の両輪となっています。

その点をくわしく紹介したく、2006 年に出版した「おいしい串揚げの本」( 第 4 版まで増刷 ) に、「串の坊 Special」にて毎年提供している新感覚の串揚げと、『六本木 浜藤』でお出ししている天然とらふぐ、トリュフ＆キャビアの料理を加えて大幅に内容を刷新しました。

『串の坊』の伝統的な串揚げとともに、こんな串揚げもあるのか、こんなふぐ料理があるのかと、串揚げとふぐ料理の斬新な魅力、新しい世界を堪能していただけたらと思います。

株式会社 串の坊 代表取締役 **乾　晴彦**

# Contents

# Kushinobo Special

| | | |
|---|---|---|
| 025 |  | ***240 Million Eyes Reiwa Ver.***<br>二億四千万の瞳 令和 ver. |
| 026 |  | ***Fresh Shiitake Mushroom, Red Snapper***<br>***with Sesame Sauce*** (*Sushi Karaku*)<br>生椎茸、鯛の胡麻和合 （鮨 加楽久） |
| 027 |  | ***White Asparagus Soup*** (*from Hokkaido*),<br>***Hamaguri Clam***<br>ホワイトアスパラガス（北海道）のスープ、地蛤 （九十九里） |
| 028 |  | ***White Shrimp, Egg, Caviar & Avocado*** (*Wakugin*)<br>白海老、卵、キャビア＆アボガド （*Wakugin*） |
| 029 |  | ***Hard Clam from Kujukuri Clam Chowder*** (*O.T.*)<br>九十九里浜の地蛤 クラムチャウダー （*O.T.*） |
| 030 |  | ***Abalone, Shark Fin Sauce***<br>鮑、フカヒレソース |
| 031 |  | ***Abalone, Liver Sauce***<br>鮑、肝ソース |
| 032 |  | ***Hozan Pork Rolled Cabbage***<br>(*Kagoshima, Nishi Sake Brewery*)<br>宝山豚 ロールキャベツ （鹿児島 西酒造） |
| 033 |  | ***Hozan Pork, Tomato Sauce***<br>(*Kagoshima, Nish Sake Brewery*)<br>宝山豚、トマトソース （鹿児島 西酒造） |

| 034 |  | ***Black Vinegar Sweet & Sour Pork***<br>***(Kagoshima, Nishi Sake Brewery)***<br>黒酢酢豚 （鹿児島 西酒造） |
| 035 |  | ***Red Vinegar Sweet & Sour Pork***<br>***(Kagoshima, Nishi Sake Brewery)***<br>赤酢酢豚 （鹿児島 西酒造） |
| 036 |  | ***Kelp with Herring Roe, Ezo Bafun Sea Urchin***<br>子持ち昆布 馬糞雲丹 |
| 037 |  | ***Scallop with Tomato Jelly & Bottarga***<br>貝柱トマトジュレ 唐墨 |
| 038 |  | ***Shark Fin***<br>フカヒレ |
| 039 |  | ***Hairy Crab, Sea Urchin, Caviar & Avocado***<br>毛蟹、雲丹、キャビア＆アボカド |
| 040 |  | ***Tuna Marinated in Soy Souce,***<br>***Konowata*** *(salted entrails of sea cucumber),*<br>***Perilla*** *(Komatsu Yasuke)*<br>鮪漬け、海鼠腸、ペリーラ （小松弥助） |
| 041 |  | ***Fugu, Caviar, White Truffles***<br>河豚、キャビア、白トリュフ （六本木浜藤） |
| 042 |  | ***Fugu, Caviar, Black Truffles***<br>河豚、キャビア、黒トリュフ （六本木浜藤） |

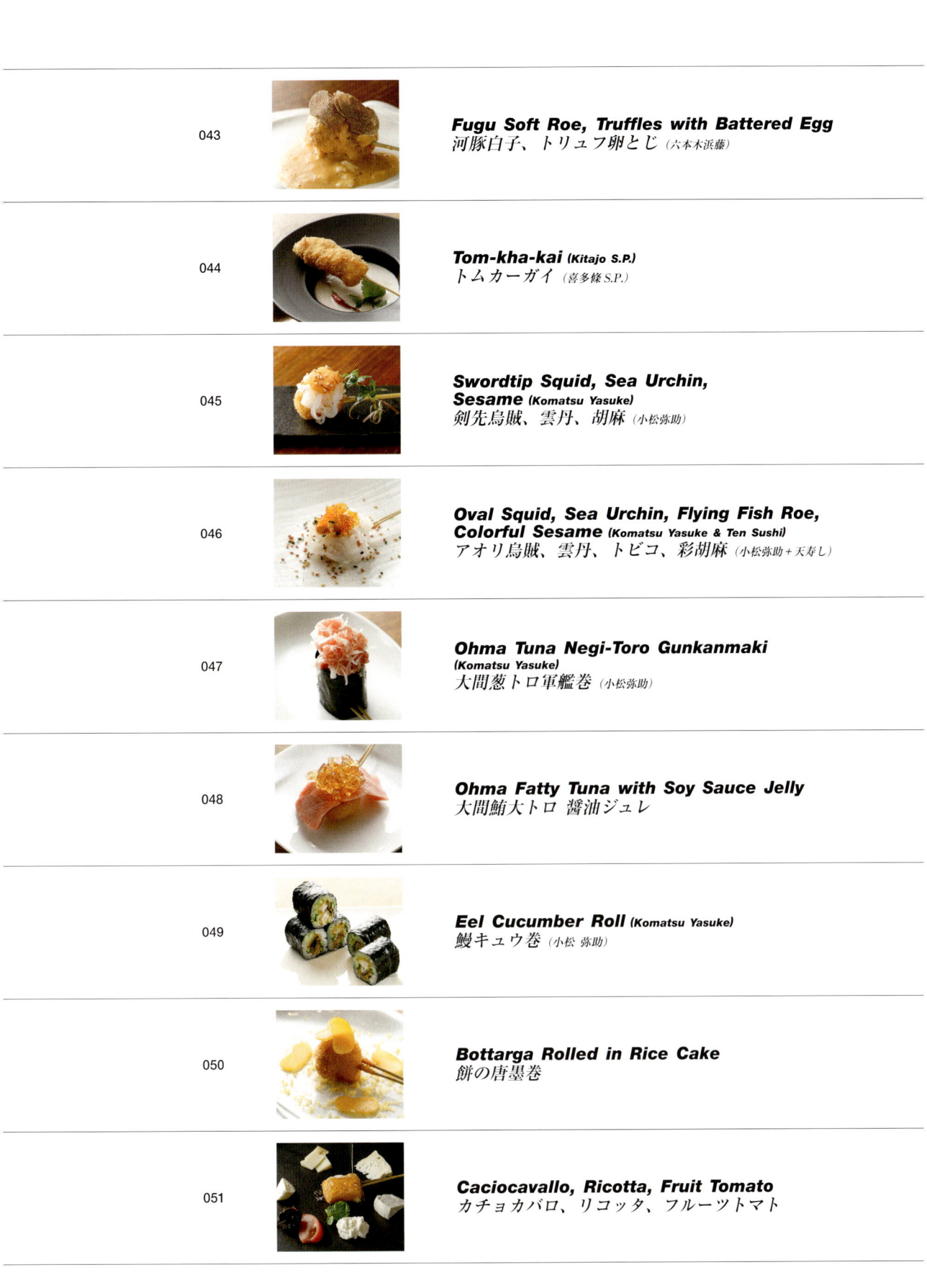

**043** Fugu Soft Roe, Truffles with Battered Egg
河豚白子、トリュフ卵とじ（六本木浜藤）

**044** Tom-kha-kai **(Kitajo S.P.)**
トムカーガイ（喜多條 S.P.）

**045** Swordtip Squid, Sea Urchin, Sesame **(Komatsu Yasuke)**
剣先烏賊、雲丹、胡麻（小松弥助）

**046** Oval Squid, Sea Urchin, Flying Fish Roe, Colorful Sesame **(Komatsu Yasuke & Ten Sushi)**
アオリ烏賊、雲丹、トビコ、彩胡麻（小松弥助＋天寿し）

**047** Ohma Tuna Negi-Toro Gunkanmaki **(Komatsu Yasuke)**
大間葱トロ軍艦巻（小松弥助）

**048** Ohma Fatty Tuna with Soy Sauce Jelly
大間鮪大トロ 醤油ジュレ

**049** Eel Cucumber Roll **(Komatsu Yasuke)**
鰻キュウ巻（小松 弥助）

**050** Bottarga Rolled in Rice Cake
餅の唐墨巻

**051** Caciocavallo, Ricotta, Fruit Tomato
カチョカバロ、リコッタ、フルーツトマト

# Varieties of *kushinobo*

| | | |
|---|---|---|
| 056 103 | | **SHRIMP** 芝海老紫蘇巻 |
| 057 | | **BEEF TENDERLOIN** 牛フィレ肉 |
| 058 104 | | **LOTUS ROOT** 蓮根 |
| 059 | | **SHIITAKE MUSHROOM** 椎茸 |
| 060 | | **AOYAGI SCALLOPS** 小柱 |
| 061 105 | | **ASPARAGUS** アスパラ |
| 062 | | **OYSTER** 牡蠣 |
| 064 106 | | **STUFFED CHICKEN WING** 手羽先 |

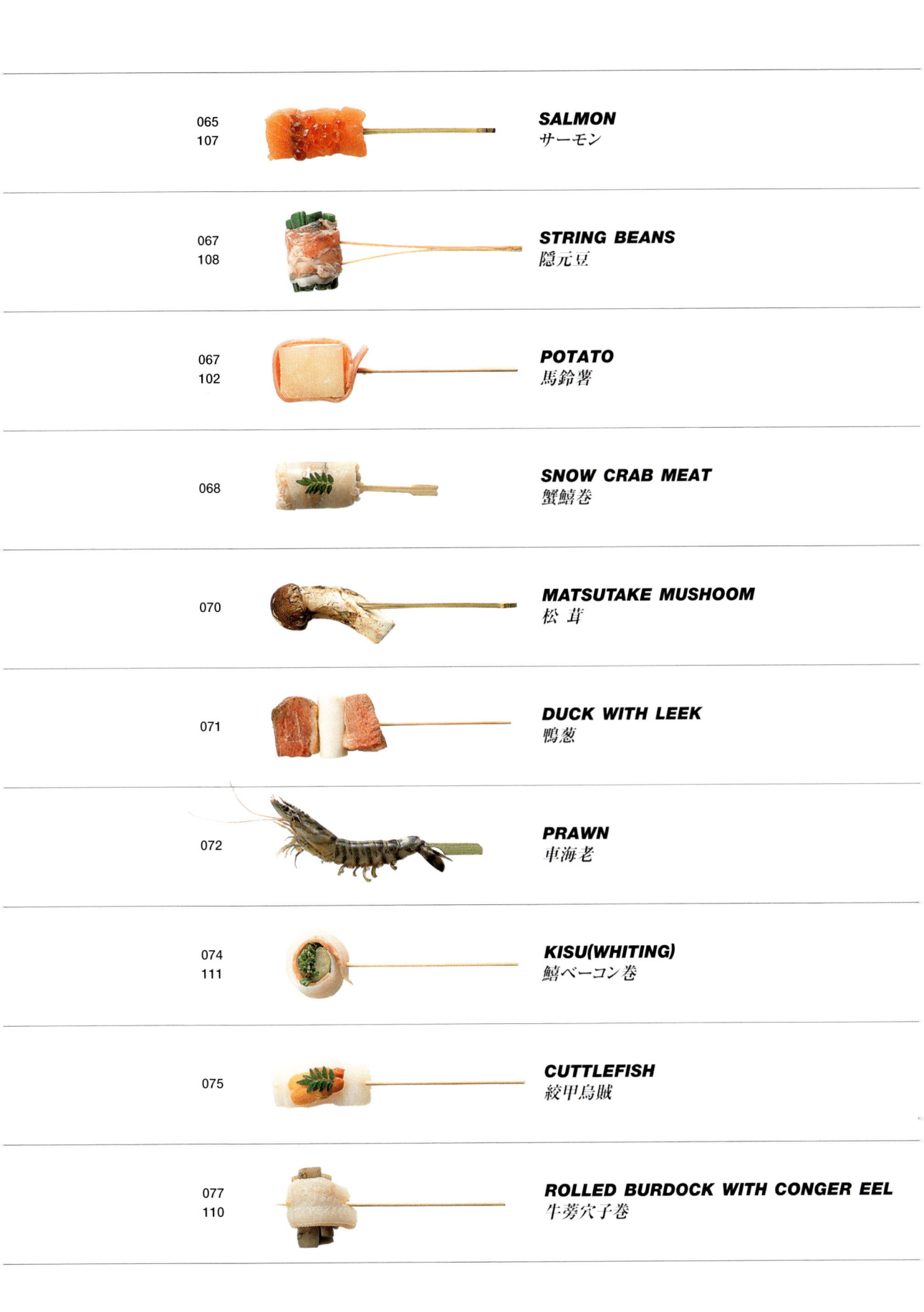

| | | |
|---|---|---|
| 065<br>107 | | **SALMON**<br>サーモン |
| 067<br>108 | | **STRING BEANS**<br>隠元豆 |
| 067<br>102 | | **POTATO**<br>馬鈴薯 |
| 068 | | **SNOW CRAB MEAT**<br>蟹鱚巻 |
| 070 | | **MATSUTAKE MUSHOOM**<br>松 茸 |
| 071 | | **DUCK WITH LEEK**<br>鴨葱 |
| 072 | | **PRAWN**<br>車海老 |
| 074<br>111 | | **KISU(WHITING)**<br>鱚ベーコン巻 |
| 075 | | **CUTTLEFISH**<br>絞甲烏賊 |
| 077<br>110 | | **ROLLED BURDOCK WITH CONGER EEL**<br>牛蒡穴子巻 |

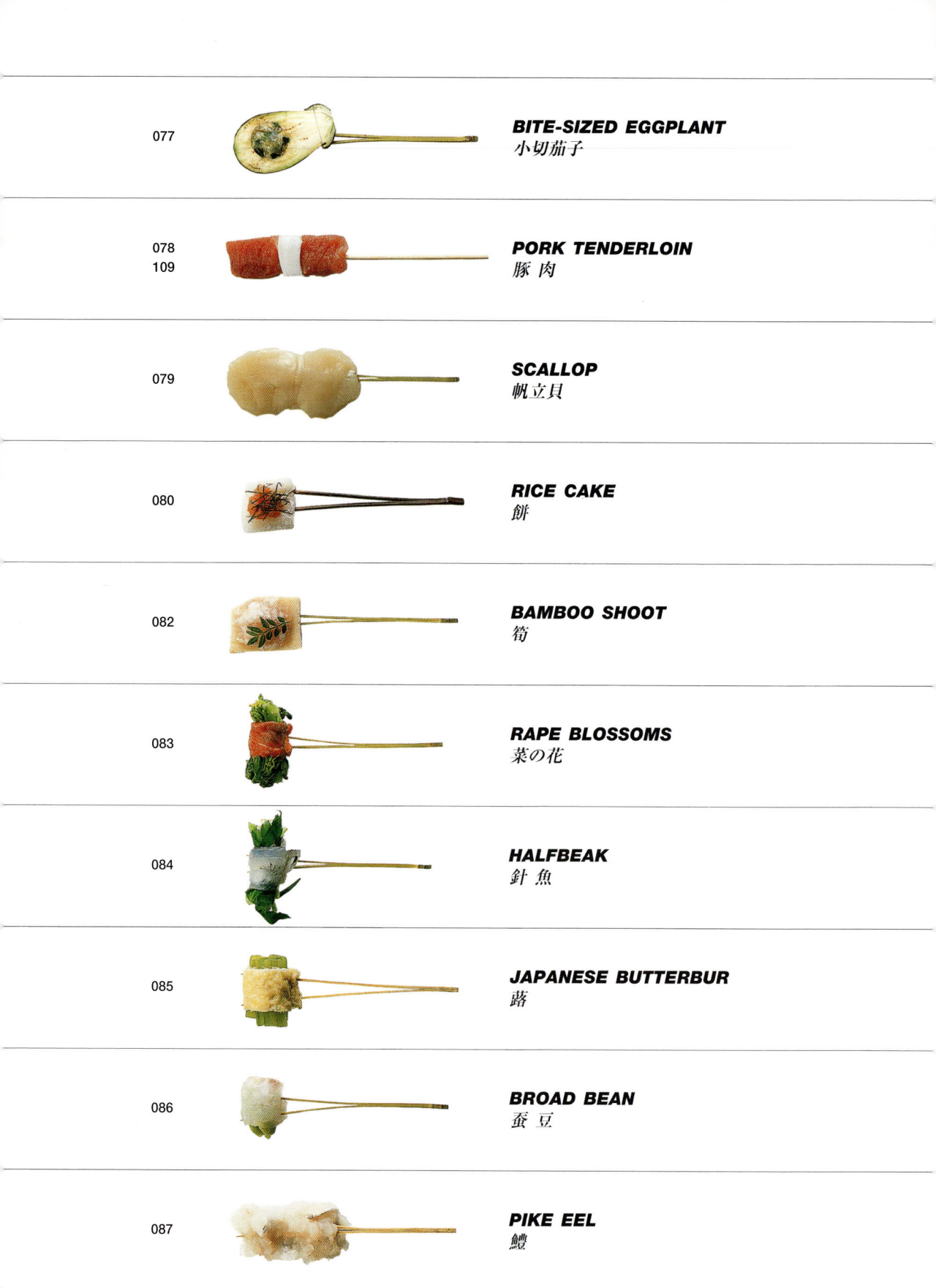

077     **BITE-SIZED EGGPLANT**
小切茄子

078
109     **PORK TENDERLOIN**
豚 肉

079     **SCALLOP**
帆立貝

080     **RICE CAKE**
餅

082     **BAMBOO SHOOT**
筍

083     **RAPE BLOSSOMS**
菜の花

084     **HALFBEAK**
針 魚

085     **JAPANESE BUTTERBUR**
蕗

086     **BROAD BEAN**
蚕 豆

087     **PIKE EEL**
鱧

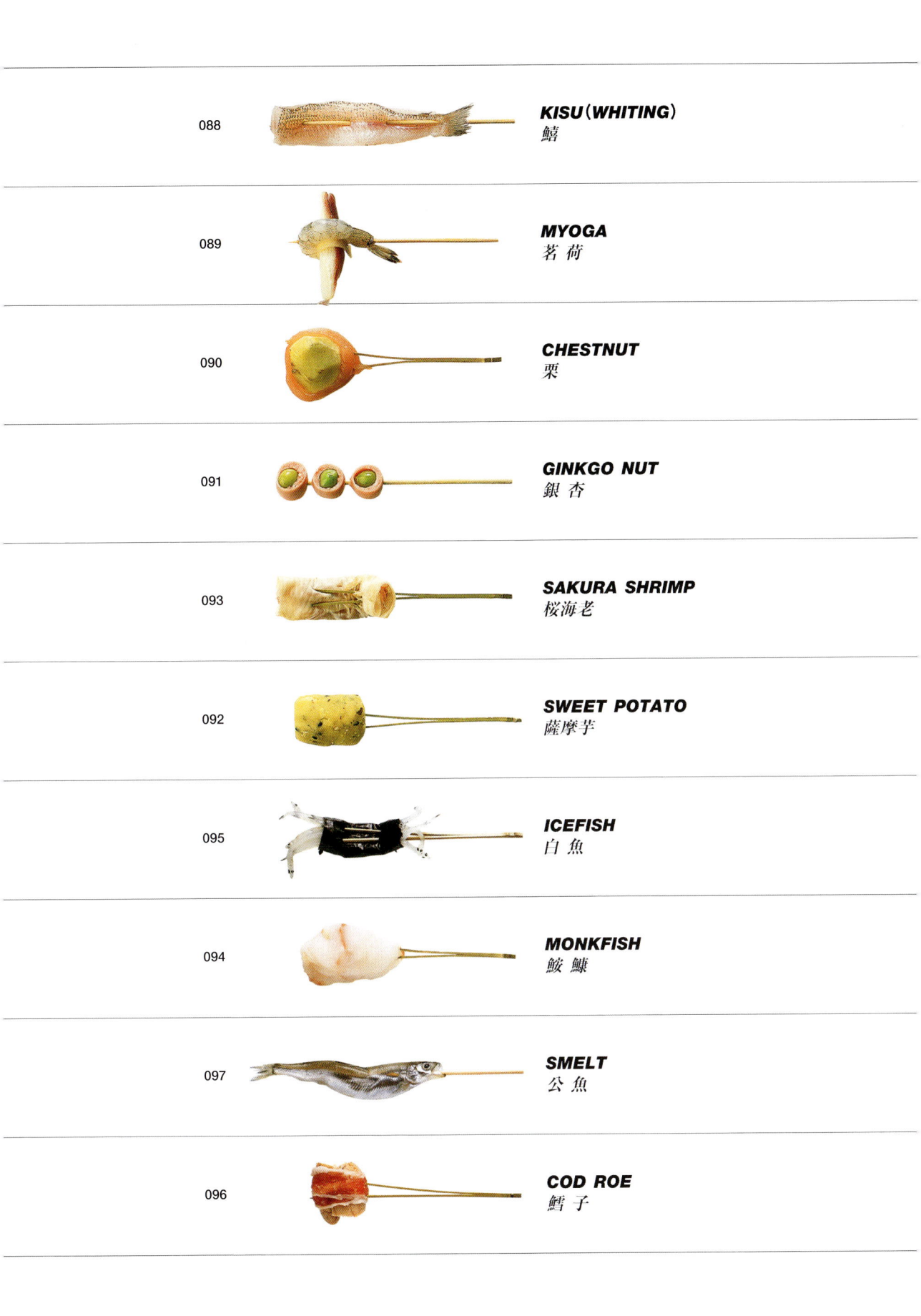

**088** KISU (WHITING) 鱚

**089** MYOGA 茗 荷

**090** CHESTNUT 栗

**091** GINKGO NUT 銀 杏

**093** SAKURA SHRIMP 桜海老

**092** SWEET POTATO 薩摩芋

**095** ICEFISH 白 魚

**094** MONKFISH 鮟 鱇

**097** SMELT 公 魚

**096** COD ROE 鱈 子

# Let kushinobo be popular all over the world!

「kushinobo」という料理を世界に。

Mr.Inui in Sri Lanka

In 2002, I went to Sri Lanka to teach the ches of the "Tree of Life Hotel" how to cook *kushinobo*, deep-fried morsels on bamboo skewers. I took panko (bread crumbs) and various sauces for *kushinobo* recipes. Somehow I managed to cook what looked like *kushinobo* but the taste wasn't quite the same (because of the foreign atmosphere of Sri Lanka? Well, perhaps). The next day I went to the market and bought some local ingredients to try *kushinobo* once more but this time with a curry flavour. Curry is part of the Sri Lankan diet. I made kushiage in Sri Lankan style. It was a big hit and gave me the idea that there should be different ways to enjoy *kushinobo* from country to country.

In 2005, I went to Kenya to teach *kushinobo* recipes to the chef of the Mpata Safari Club. I had nothing prepared for my *kushinobo* recipes except some freshly-caught fish from Lake Victoria. Consequently, I used cocktail sticks instead of skewers and put the fish and some meat and vegetables (which were available in the hotel kitchen at that time) on the cocktail sticks. I served my *kushinobo* with a fondue-based sauce (admittedly my improvised version). It was a big success!

We have opened *kushinobo* branches in the US, Singapore, Hong Kong and Taiwan. Unfortunately, none of these were success-ful, because I was preoccupied with intro-ducing the true taste of traditional Japanese

2002年にスリランカのホテル「Tree of Life」のシェフに串揚げを教えたことがあります。

日本から持っていったパン粉、ソースなどの材料で作りました。ほぼ日本の串揚げに近いものができましたが、現地で食べると、どこか違和感がありました。翌日、市場に行き、現地の食材を使って串揚げを作りました。そして、スリランカで日常的に食べられているカレーを串揚げにかけてみました。いわば、串揚げのスリランカ・スタイルです。

これが大好評でした。これを見て、串揚げは国ごとの楽しみ方があるはずだと確信したのでした。

2005年には、ケニアのホテル「ムパタ・サファリ・クラブ」のシェフに串揚げを教えました。ビクトリア湖で釣った魚を串揚げにしたのですが、何も準備をしていなかったので、爪楊枝に魚の他、ホテルのキッチンにあった肉や野菜などを刺して揚げました。このホテルのレストランの料理はフレンチ。串揚げはフォンドヴォーをベースに即席で作ったソースでいただきました。これは大好評でした。

実はこれまでに、アメリカやシンガポール、香港、台湾に『串の坊』を出店したことがあります。

しかし、どれも長続きしませんでした。単に串に刺して油で揚げるのではなく、四季

kushinobo, which is not just deep-fried skewered food but also ingeniously uses different ingredients that represent the wonderful flavours of the four seasons. I didn't stop to consider the various cultural environments and different eating habits.

I then gradually discovered that kushinobo can be very popular with non-Japanese audiences when ingredients and deep-frying oils from their own countries are used. I now believe that adding a little twist to the traditional Japanese kushinobo cooking to please non-Japanese palates is the best way to spread this wonderful feature of Japanese food culture. My invaluable experience led me to compile my ideas and inspiration for kushinobo cooking into this book.

In Japan, some argue that deep-fried skewered food is called kushikatsu in the West and kushiage in the East. My dream is that one day this wonderful deep-fried skewered food will be recognized as kushinobo by the entire world. Therefore, I have taken the liberty of using the term kushinobo instead of kushiage in this book. Since my visits to Sri Lanka and Kenya, "kushinobo" has been added to the restaurant menus of the Tree of Life Hotel and the Mpata Safari Club.

の材料に工夫を凝らして揚げる歴史ある日本の料理を、海外で同じものが味わえるように努力しましたが、食文化や環境の違いでうまくいかなかったのです。

ところが、その国々の材料、油を利用して、串に刺して揚げると、たいへん喜ばれるのです。日本で料理されている串揚げをそのままではなく、串揚げのスタイルでその国の材料を味わってもらうことが、串揚げの文化を広める近道だと思いました。この様な経緯が本書の出版へと至らせました。

日本では、関西では「串カツ」と呼び、関東では「串揚げ」と呼ぶという論議はありますが、世界では、串に刺して揚げて食べる料理は「kushinobo」と呼ばれるようになるのが私の夢です。スリランカの「Tree of Life」やケニアの「ムパタ・サファリ・クラブ」には「kushinobo」がメニューに加わりました。

そんな願いもあって、本書は世界中の人が読めるように英語と日本語の対訳にしました。英訳では「串揚げ」を「Japannese crumbed deep-fried skewers」等と訳さないで、ずばり「kushinobo」といたします。

Mr.Inui in Kenya

# Kushinobo Special

Every year in eary summer, we host an event called Kushinobo Special in Ginza, Tokyo. We try and create new ideas each year because many of our guests at Kushinobo Special come back every year.

毎年、新緑の季節になると、東京・銀座店で「串の坊　Special」を出すイベントを開催します。
毎年来店してくださるお客様がほとんどですので、楽しんでいただくために毎年模索しています。

# What is
# Kushinobo Special?

## 串の坊 Special とは？

Every year in early summer, we host an event called Kushinobo Special in Ginza, Tokyo. For two weeks, I personally stand in the kitchen to cook and serve the 16 different kinds of *kushinobo* to our guests.

This is an event we started in 2012, where we consider each skewer as one dish and express various cuisines in a form of *kushinobo*. In 2012 and 2013, we held this event for four days, with different 16 menus every day, because we had guests who came in every day. We soon had good reviews and extended the event from four days to two weeks. However, we still did not have enough seats for our guests. Since 2017, we hold this event twice each day, for two weeks. Thankfully the year 2019 was fully booked and we welcomed over 500 guests in two weeks.

The 16 *kushinobo* menus include 12 lavish ingredients, three "sushinobo" (kushinobo-style sushi), and a cheese *kushinobo* using cheese from Yoshida Farm. We changed the menus for the first three years. We kept the popular ones, improved the previous ones, and now we provide previous and new menus all together. To provide the sense of a set menu, we carefully think about in what order we serve the *kushinobo*, and I feel that in 2017, we were able to complete the whole course. In 2018, we composed a menu without

毎年新緑の頃になると、東京・銀座店で「串の坊 Special」のイベントを開催します。2 週間、社長の私自身が揚げ、16 種類の串揚げを提供します。

串揚げ 1 本 1 本を料理として考え、様々な料理を串揚げで表現するのが「串の坊 Special」。 2012 年から始め、2012 年と 2013 年は 4 日間の開催で、出す 16 種類は当初は毎日変えていました。毎日来る人がいたからです。評判が高まり、2016 年からは開催期間を 2 週間にしましたがまだ席が足らず、2017 年からは完全 2 部制にしました。2019 年も満員御礼で 2 週間で 500 名を超えるお客様が来店しました。

16 種類の串揚げの内容は、12 種類の高級食材を使った串揚げ、寿司を串揚げにした「寿司の坊」が 3 本、そして吉田牧場のチーズの串揚げ 1 本です。最初の 3 年間くらいは毎年内容を全部変えていましたが、好評だったものは残したり、また、前年に出したものをバージョンアップさせたり、いまは新旧織り交ぜて出します。コースとして楽しめるよう、出す順番やバランスも考えてお出しします。2017 年にほぼコースとして完成した感はあります。また、2018 年よりソースをつけて食べない串揚げのみで 16 種

using any sauce. I come up with new *kushinobo* ideas while I'm jogging, and my chefs come up with unique ideas as well. There are menus that I thought of while I was at a concert. Some of the dishes introduced at Kushinobo Special are later incorporated into Kushinobo restaurants' menus. We try and create new ideas because many of our guests at Kushinobo Special come back every year.

We started Kushinobo Special as a remembrance to Keiji Ohta. He was a director of Ginza Kushinobo, who was always progressive and keen to create new ideas. Unfortunately, he fought and lost to the battle to leukemia. To inherit what he had left for us and to continue his legacy, I personally invited those who shared similar hopes and started this event to serve special *kushinobo*. That was in June of 2012.

Thankfully this has become a significant and meaningful event, at the same time raising our employees' motivations as well.

類は構成しました。これまで提供した串揚げは、大部分は私が考えていますが、中にはスタッフがアイデアを出したものもあります。ジョギング中にひらめいたものも多いです。奥田民生のコンサートの演奏中にひらめいたものもあります。この「串の坊 Special 」で出したものから取捨選択して『串の坊』全店のメニューに反映もさせています。

「串の坊 Special 」は毎年来店してくださるお客様がほとんどですので、楽しんでいただくために毎回模索します。

串の坊 Special のイベントは、きっかけは、この銀座店の店長の であった太田敬二君を偲んで始めたものです。努力家で新しい工夫をすることにも積極的な彼でしたが、急性白血病の闘病の末、帰らぬ人となりました。太田敬二君の頑張りを無駄にしないよう、彼の足跡を残していけるよう、社長の私自らが追悼のためにこの意義を理解していただけるお客様を招き、特別な串揚げを揚げるイベントを組んだのが 2012 年の 6 月でした。

おかげさまで、『串の坊』にとってもとても意義のあるイベントに育ち、商品開発に対する従業員の意識も高まりました。

# Chinese Yam Rolled in Yuba (tofu skin), Sea Urchin, Pickled Tuna, Seaweed, Japanese Yam (Komatsu Yasuke)

*This is an homage to a sushi served by Kazuo Morita at restaurant ''Komatsu Yasuke'' in Kanazawa. The glass plate is a work by Taizo Yasuda.*

## 長芋の湯葉巻、雲丹、鮪漬け、海苔、大和芋 (小松 弥助)

金沢の「小松弥助」の森田一夫氏定番の逸品をオマージュしました。盛り付けの硝子食器は安田泰三氏の作品です。

### *Beef Stew (Tochigi Beef Ribeye)*

*Fried beef ribeye with house-made demi-glace sauce.*

### ビーフシチュー（栃木牛リブ芯）

牛肉のリブ芯を揚げて、自家製のデミグラスソースをかけました。

# Special Sendai Beef Chuck Flap

*Fried premium Sendai Beef loin with basil sauce.*

## 特選仙台牛ザブトン バジルソース

仙台牛の特上ロースを揚げて、バジルソースを添えました。

# *Corn*

*Fried morning-picked corn with rich corn soup.*

## トウモロコシ

朝もぎのトウモロコシを揚げて、コクのあるコーンスープとともに味わってもらいます。

## *"Torishiki-nobo"* Chicken Heart, Meatballs, Thigh, Gizzard (Meguro)

*At the 60th birthday (and his 40th anniversary as a singer-songwriter) party of Tatsuo Kamon, Yoshiki Ikegawa of "Torishiki" and I collaborated to create a dish with we fried chicken heart, meatball, thigh, gizzard, on one skewer. This is its replication. We arranged their sauce with egg yolk.*

### 鳥しきの坊 ハツ、つくね、腿肉、砂肝 (目黒)

嘉門タツオ氏の還暦＆芸能生活40周年記念パーティーの料理で、「鳥しき」の御主人池川義輝氏とコラボして作った、「鳥しき」の串ネタのハツ、つくね、腿肉、砂肝を少しずつ串に刺し、焼かずに揚げると云う料理を再現しました。タレは鳥しきの照タレに卵黄を混ぜました。

## Sukiyaki (Ue wo Muite Arukou)

*Fried beef with sukiyaki sauce; hence the naming. Served with egg yolk sauce.*

### 上を向いて歩こう

牛肉を揚げて、割り下とともに。すき焼き味なので、「上を向いて歩こう」というネーミングです。卵黄ソースをかけて提供します。

## 240 Million Eyes Heisei Ver.

*This kushinobo was created in Heisei Era for Hiromi Go, who has been our guest at Kushinobo Special every year. To actualize his hit song "240 Million Eyes", we fried two soft-boiled quale eggs to represent the eyes and added plenty of caviar.*

### 二億四千万の瞳　平成 ver.

毎回御来店戴いている郷ひろみさんの為に平成時代に考案した一品です。「二億四千万の瞳」と云う代表曲を串カツで具現化するために、うずら卵を二つ半熟にして揚げて瞳に見立て、その上にキャビアをふんだんに載せてそれを表現しました。

### 240 Million Eyes Reiwa Ver.

*With the start of a new era, we created the Reiwa version of "240 Million Eyes". We cut the kelp with herring roe into two round pieces, fried them on skewers, topped them with sea urchin with plenty of caviar. It comes with a message; "Count the eggs on the kelp, sea urchin, and caviar with a microscope. There are exactly 240 million of them."*

### 二億四千万の瞳 令和 ver.

新しい令和時代の到来に、二億四千万の瞳令和 ver. を考えました。子持ち昆布を丸くカットして二つ串に刺して揚げ、それぞれに雲丹をのせてキャビアをふんだんにトッピングします。「子持ち昆布と雲丹、キャビアを顕微鏡を使って、キチンと数えると丁度二億四千万あります。」という言葉を添えて。

# Fresh Shiitake Mushroom, Red Snapper with Sesame Sauce (Sushi Karaku)

*Fried shiitake mushroom is topped with sesame-seasoned red snapper, a classic at "Sushi Karaku" in Ginza.*

## 生椎茸、鯛の胡麻和合（鮨 加楽久）

生椎茸を揚げて、銀座「鮨　加樂久」の名物「鯛の胡麻和合」をのせました。

## White Asparagus Soup (from Hokkaido), Hamaguri Clam

*After tasting the amazing white asparagus soup in a restaurant by Rhine River in Germany, this was an immediate addition to our menu. Fried hard clams are scattered over the soup like croutons.*

### ホワイトアスパラガスのスープ、地蛤 （北海道）

春、ドイツのライン川の辺のレストランで食べたホワイトアスパラガスのスープに感動して早速オンメニューしました。地蛤を揚げ、それをスープにクルトン代わりの雰囲気で入れて召し上がる料理です。

# White Shrimp, Egg, Caviar & Avocado (Wakugin)

*Tetsuya Wakuda (owner/chef of "Tetsuya's" in Sydney) opened "Wakugin" in Singapore. I visited him in 2010 and was amazed by how a frozen egg yolk could be so rich in taste. I had to add this egg kushinobo to our menu.*

## 白海老、卵、キャビア＆アボガド (Wakugin)

シドニーのレストラン「Tetsuya's」のオーナーシェフ和久田哲也氏が、シンガポールで出店した「Wakugin」で、2010年に来訪した際、冷凍卵の黄身がこんなにもコクがあって美味しくなるものかと感動し、以後この卵を使った串カツを一品リストアップしています。

### Hard Clam from Kujukuri Clam Chowder (O.T.)

*O.T. stands for Tamio Okuda (Japanese singer-songwriter). While I was at his concert, I remembered how Okuda and Yosui Inoue (Japanese singer-songwriter) did a wonderful concert years ago. From there, I remembered Inoue once said on TV how he likes clam chowder. I came up with this menu while I was at Okuda's concert.*

### 九十九里浜の地蛤 クラムチャウダー (O.T.)

O.T. とは、奥田民生さんのこと。2018 年の奥田民生さんのコンサートの途中で、「民生さんと陽水さんのライブ懐かしいなあ」と思い出し、そこから、陽水さんはクラムチャウダーが好きだってテレビで言っていたことを思い出し、奥田民生さんのコンサート中にひらめいて完成させた串揚げです。

### Abalone, Shark Fin Sauce

*We use abalone in our menu every year to offer a sense of luxury. In 2019, we served it with shark fin sauce to give a Chinese touch.*

### 鮑、フカヒレソース

プレミアム感を醸し出すために、鮑を用いた料理は必ず入れるようにしていますが、2019 年は鮑にフカヒレソースを掛けて中華のスタイルにしました。

# Abalone, Liver Sauce

*Fried abalone with sauce made from its liver.*

## 鮑、肝ソース

鮑を揚げて、鮑の肝で作ったソースを合わせました。

# Hozan Pork Rolled Cabbage
## (Kagoshima, Nishi Sake Brewery)

*Hozan pork is raised on potatoes used to brew "Tomino Hozan" at Nishi Sake Brewing Co.,Ltd. Enjoy it with white sauce.*

## 宝山豚 ロールキャベツ （鹿児島 西酒造）

鹿児島の「富乃宝山」の蔵元・西酒造で蒸留した後の芋で育てた黒豚が宝山豚。ロールキャベツのソースをかけました。

### Hozan Pork,
### Tomato Sauce (Kagoshima, Nish Sake Brewery)

*Black pork raised on potatoes to brew shochu is fried, served with tomato sauce for an Italian touch.*

## 宝山豚、トマトソース (鹿児島 西酒造)

「宝山豚」を揚げ、トマトソースをかけてイタリアン風にしました。

## Black Vinegar Sweet & Sour Pork
### (Kagoshima, Nishi Sake Brewery)

*Black "Hozan Pork" raised on left over sake lees after brewing shochu is fried, served with sweet & sour sauce. The sauce is made with black vinegar.*

### 黒酢酢豚 （鹿児島 西酒造）

「宝山豚」を揚げて、酢豚のタレをかけました。これは黒酢のバージョンです。

### Red Vinegar Sweet & Sour Pork
**(Kagoshima, Nishi Sake Brewery)**

*Sweet & sour pork with red vinegar sauce.*

### 赤酢酢豚（鹿児島 西酒造）
左ページの「黒酢酢豚」のタレを赤酢で作ったバージョンです。

### Kelp with Herring Roe, Ezo Bafun Sea Urchin

*A classic at Kushinobo, "Kelp with Herring Roe" is topped with plenty of sea urchin. Enjoy the umami and texture of sea urchin.*

### 子持ち昆布 馬糞雲丹

「串の坊」の名物の一つ、「子持ち昆布」に雲丹をたっぷりのせました。食感と旨味とともに味わってもらう串揚げです。

# Scallop with Tomato Jelly Bottarga

*Fried scallop is topped with tomato jelly, bottarga graded on top. Saltiness of bottarga brings out the sweetness in scallops.*

## 貝柱トマトジュレ 唐墨

帆立貝柱を揚げ、トマトジュレをのせました。上から唐墨をすりおろしてかけます。
唐墨の塩気が帆立の甘みを引き立てます。

## *Shark Fin*

*Shark fin soup is poured over fried shark fin. Bok choy and meaty shiitake mushroom on the side.*

## フカヒレ

フカヒレを揚げて、フカヒレスープをかけます。青梗菜と椎茸を付け合わせに。

### Hairy Crab, Sea Urchin, Caviar & Avocado

*Fried avocado is topped with hairy crab, sea urchin, and caviar. Many guests are surprised by this layered flavor.*

### 毛蟹、雲丹、キャビア＆アボカド

アボカドを揚げて、上に毛蟹、雲丹、キャビアを重ねました。重層的な味わいに、驚かれる方が多いです。

# Tuna Marinated in Soy Souce, Konowata (salted entrails of sea cucumber), Perilla

*"Sushinobo" is a kushinobo with fried shari (sushi rice) and sushi topping. We ask "Ginza Sushi Kohonten" to prepare the shari everyday during this event; we then skewer and fry them. 2019 theme was "Komatsu Yasuke" (sushi restaurant in Kanazawa). We prepare the sauce for pickled tuna in a Baccarat bowl. Top the fried shari with Japanese pepper, pickled tuna, konowata, and perilla, just like how "Yasuke" does it. Picture below is an arrangement of "Komatsu Yasuke & Sushi Karaku" with pickled tuna.*

## 鮪漬け、海鼠腸、ペリーラ（小松弥助）

「寿司の坊」は、鮨のシャリを揚げてネタをのせて召し上がる鮨のような串揚げです。「銀座寿司幸本店」さんに開催期間中は毎日、串揚げ用に小さくシャリを握っていただき、それを串に刺して揚げます。2019 年のテーマは「小松弥助」。弥助さんと同じようにバカラの器に漬けタレを仕込み、揚げたシャリに山葵、鮪漬け、海鼠腸、ペリーラをのせました。写真下は、鮪漬けを和えた小松弥助＆鮨加樂久のアレンジです。

## *Fugu, Caviar, White Truffles*

*This is one of the most luxurious menus at Kushinobo Special. We serve this only in November and December when white truffles are available.*

## 河豚、キャビア、白トリュフ

串の坊 Special の中でも最上級の串揚げの一つです。白トリュフを提供できる 11 月〜 12 月限定の串揚げです。

## *Fugu, Caviar, Black Truffles*

*Fried fugu with black truffles and caviar; the new top three delicacies of the world.*

## 河豚、キャビア、黒トリュフ

河豚を揚げて、黒トリュフとキャビアを合わせた、新世界3大珍味の共演です。

# Fugu Soft Roe, Truffles with Battered Egg

*Fried fugu together with battered egg. Topping it with plenty of white and black truffles.*

## 河豚白子、トリュフ卵とじ

河豚の白子を揚げて、卵とじの地と合わせました。さらに白トリュフと黒トリュフを合わせてを贅沢にトッピングしました。

### Tom-kha-kai (Kitajo S.P.)

*This tom-kha-kai is made by Thai cooking expert Terumi Kitajo, who is the wife of Tadashi Kitajo, the chairman of Japan Lyricist Association. Her soup is served with chicken wing meat skewered and fried together with celery. Like any other Kushinobo Special soup, dip your kushinobo in the soup and enjoy.*

### トムカーガイ (喜多條 S.P.)

タイ料理研究家で、日本作詞家協会会長の喜多條忠氏の奥様、輝美さんが作ったスープ、トムカーガイに、鳥の手羽先の身をせせってセロリと共に刺した串揚げを合わせました。他の串の坊 Special のスープと同様、基本的に串揚げをスープに落とし込んで召し上がっていただきます。

### Swordtip Squid, Sea Urchin, Sesame (Komatsu Yasuke)

*Fried shari served with "Komatsu Yasuke" style swordtip squid and sea urchin, decorated with bofu (dropwort plant).*

### 剣先烏賊、雲丹、胡麻 (小松弥助)

銀シャリを揚げた上に、「小松弥助」風の剣先烏賊、雲丹をのせ、防風を飾りました。

## Oval Squid, Sea Urchin, Flying Fish Roe, Colorful Sesame (Komatsu Yasuke & Tenzushi)

*Squid is filleted into three pieces then minced, like how it's done at "Komatsu Yasuke". Served together with sea urchin, flying fish roe and colorful sesame, associating it with the squid served at Tenzushi in Kokura, Fukuoka.*

### アオリ烏賊、雲丹、トビコ、彩胡麻 (小松弥助 + 天寿し)

「小松弥助」風のアオリ烏賊を三枚に下ろし刻み、盛り付けは、雲丹、トビコ、彩胡麻を添えて小倉の「天寿司」の烏賊を連想させました。

# Ohma Tuna Negi-Toro Gunkanmaki
## (Komatsu Yasuke)

*Fatty tuna cut and mixed together with white leek on the cutting board, and we have Yasuke-style negi-toro.*

### 大間葱トロ軍艦巻 （小松弥助）

大トロを切り、白髪ネギと合わせ、まな板の上で出刃包丁でトントンと叩いて作るネギトロ弥助風です。

# *Ohma Fatty Tuna  Soy Sauce Jelly*

*Fried shari topped with Ohma's fatty tuna, served with soy sauce jelly.*

## 大間鮪大トロ 醤油ジュレ

銀シャリを揚げた上に大間の鮪の大トロを。醤油のジュレと合わせて召し上がって
いただきます。

### *Eel Cucumber Roll* (*Komatsu Yasuke*)

*2019 was the year Mr. Kazuo Morita from "Komatsu Yasuke" visited our restaurant as our guest, and I wanted to add this to the menu as an homage and spent quite some time on it. Fried eel and cucumber are wrapped in seaweed like Temaki-sushi (hand-rolled sushi).*

### 鰻キュウ巻 (小松弥助)

*2019 年は金沢の「小松弥助」の森田一夫氏がご来店ということでしたので、どうしても鰻キュウをリストに入れたくて一番悩んだ料理です。揚げた鰻と胡瓜を、海苔で手巻き寿司風に仕立てました。*

### Bottarga Rolled in Rice Cake

*House-made bottarga rolled in freshly made rice cake is fried, with bottarga topping.*

### 餅の唐墨巻

自家製の唐墨につき立ての餅を巻いて揚げ、さらに唐墨をトッピングします。

# *Caciocavallo, Ricotta, Fruit Tomato*

*Caciocavallo made by Zensaku Yoshida at Yoshida Farm in Okayama is fried, drizzled with honey with ricotta cheese and fruits on the side.*

## カチョカバロ、リコッタ、フルーツトマト

岡山の吉田牧場の吉田全作氏入魂のカチョカバロチーズを揚げて蜂蜜を掛け、リコッタチーズやドライフルーツを添えます。

# Let's Enjoy Kushinobo

Kushinobo is more than just meat, fish and shellfish, and vegetables deep-fried on skewers. Each skewer is a course in itself. We have 100 seasonal recipes in our repertoire, and today you have 38 dishes to choose from. How many will you try? We'll leave it up to you.

肉や魚介や野菜を串に刺して揚げるだけではないのが、「Kushinobo」の料理、1本ずつが、一つの料理です。四季折々の串揚げ百選の中、本日の御用意は38種類。あなたが何本召し上がるかは「おまかせ」です。

# Delicious sauces for kushinobo

*We prepare 6 different dipping sauces for kushinobo. Try any of them for different types of kushinobo. You'll never grow tired of eating at Kushinobo.*

「kushinobo」では6種類の味付けを用意しています。どの串揚げにどのソースを付けるかは、あなたの好み。お好きな味付けで楽しんでください。何度食べても飽きないのが「kushinobo」です。

**Lemon**
レモン

**Sesame Mustard Sauce**
胡麻からしソース

**Mustard**
マスタード

**Ponzu**
ポン酢

**Sesame Salt** *(see page115)*
胡麻岩塩

**Kushinobo Sauce** *(see page114)*
特製ソース

# Kushinobo's salad

*Before serving kushinobo, we serve raw vegetables. See them as an amusement, a salad, or even crudites. As with kushinobo, pick them up with your fingers. Try with seasonal miso dip.*

串揚げを食べていただく前に、生野菜スティックと浅葱、季節野菜の味噌をお出しします。これはアミューズであり、サラダであり、グラニテでもあります。串揚げ同様、手でつまんで気軽に召し上がってください。

**Green Onion**
浅葱

**Cabbage**
キャベツ

**Carrot**
人参

**Cucanbar**
キュウリ

**Cherry Tomato**
プティトマト

**Miso Dip**
季節野菜の味噌

SHRIMP
芝海老紫蘇巻

## SHRIMP

*Shrimp are gently Wrapped in shiso leaves and deep fried. The wonderful aroma of shiso leaves and the sweet flavor of shrimp harmonize with the appetizing deep-fry fragrance and are infused with the magic of champagne in your mouth.*

## 芝海老紫蘇巻

芝海老を紫蘇の葉で巻いて揚げます。紫蘇の香りと蝦の甘み、フライの香ばしさが引き立て合うハーモニーを、口の中でからみ合うシャンパーニュで合わせました。

## Suggested beverage

N.V. Pierre Moncuit Campagne Chardonner 100%
シャンパーニュ　ピエールモンキュイ NV. 品種：シャルドネ 100%

# BEEF TENDERROIN

The delicate flavor of tenderloin wagyu is preserved in this simple deep-fry recipe. This prime beef fillet is enhanced by its rich gravy and the mild taste of Junmai Daiginjo made of finest rice.

## 牛フィレ肉

柔らかくて繊細な味わいの牛フィレ肉をシンプルに揚げました。ふくよかな日本酒の純米大吟醸は牛フィレ肉のジューシーな肉汁との相性が絶妙です。

BEEF TENDERLOIN
牛フィレ肉

### Suggested beverage

Sake  Juyondai Shichiju-nijukan (Junmai Dai Ginjo) Aiyama  Takagi Sake Brewery (Yamagata Pref.)

日本酒　十四代　七重二十貫（純米大吟醸）　品種：愛山　高木酒造（山形）

**LOTUS ROOT**
蓮根

**SHIITAKE MUSHROOM**
椎茸

# LOTUS ROOT

*Lotus root is stuffed with curry-flavored minced beef. The crunchiness of the lotus root and the strong curry flavor are gently complemented by aged sake.*

# 蓮 根

蓮根の穴にカレー風味の牛挽き肉を詰めました。まるでシェリーのような日本酒の熟成酒は、歯触りのよいカレー風味の蓮根の力強い風味をやさしく包み込みます。

## Suggested beverrage

Aged sake Darumamasamune (3years)　Nihonbare　Shiraki Kosuke company (Gifu Pref.)

日本酒古酒　達磨正宗（熟成３年）　品種：日本晴　白木恒助商店（岐阜）

# SHIITAKE MUSHROOM

*The meaty shiitake mushroom is stuffed with minced shrimp and topped with celery, onion, and parsley tartar sauce. The complex, profound taste of this kushinobo is complemented by distilled potato spirit soda.*

# 椎 茸

肉厚の椎茸に、海老のミンチを詰めました。セロリと玉葱、パセリのタルタルソースをトッピング。複雑で奥行きのある味わいに、樽熟成させた芋焼酎の炭酸割りを合わせました。

## Suggested beverrage

Imo-shochu　Tenshinoyuwaku　Koganesengan　Nishi Sake Brewery (Kagoshima)

芋焼酎　天使の誘惑　品種：黄金千貫　西酒造（鹿児島）

# AOYAGI SCALLOPS

Aoyagi scallops are wrapped in roasted seaweed. Champagne-like sparkling sake flavors this kushinobo with a touch of citrus, heightening the taste of the ocean.

# 小柱

青柳の小柱を海苔で巻きました。シャンパーニュのような日本酒の活性にごり酒は、ほんのり柑橘系の香りです。爽やかな味わいが磯の香りを引き立てます。

AOYAGI SCALLOPS
小柱

## Suggested beverage

Sparkling Sake Oroku Kei (Junmai ginjo) Yamadanishiki  Oroku Sake Brewery (Shimane Pref.)
日本酒　王祿 渓（純米吟醸にごり）　品種：山田錦　王祿酒造（島根）

**ASPARAGUS**
アスパラ

## *ASPARAGUS*

*Asuparagus and pork rolls. The al dente texture of the asparagus and the touch of mayonnaise go well with the flavor of Bourgogne Chardonnay.*

### アスパラ

アスパラには豚バラ肉を巻いてあります。シャキッとしたアスパラの食感とマヨネーズのほのかな酸味が、ブルゴーニュのシャルドネの樽の風味によく合います。

### Suggested beverage

White Wine　Pouilly-Fuisse (Chardonnay) Dom.Valette (Bourgogne)
白ワイン　プュイイフィッセ　品種：シャルドネ　ドメーヌ・バレット（ブルゴーニュ）

**OYSTER**
牡蠣

# OYSTER

*Oysters have a rich taste and their gorgeous flavor is emphasized when they are deep-fried. This divine seafood merge well with complex and refined champagne.*

## 牡 蠣

味わい豊かな大粒の牡蠣を揚げると、衣の中の牡蠣がさらに濃厚な味わいになり、旨さが引き立ちます。磯のごちそうには上品で複雑な極上のシャンパーニュを合わせました。

## Suggested beverage

Champagne Henri Giraud Grand Cru d'Ay Fût de Chêne Brut　Pinot Noir70〜75% Chardonnay 25〜30%
HENRI GIRAUD (Champagne)

シャンパーニュ　アンリ・ジロー・フュ・ド・シェーヌ　品種：ピノ・ノワール 70 〜 75%
シャルドネ 25 〜 30%　アンリ・ジロー（シャンパーニュ）

# STUFFED CHICKEN WING

A chicken wing is stuffed with minced shrimp and shiso leaves, and then wrapped in seaweed. The lingering taste of this kushinobo harmonizes with aromatic Awamori (distilled spirit from Okinawa region), served just with water, no ice.

## 手羽先

鶏肉の手羽先を開いて、海老のミンチと紫蘇の葉を詰め、海苔で巻いています。香ばしさのある泡盛には、主張が強いこの料理を合わせます。氷無しの水割りで。

STUFFED CHICKEN WING
手羽先

## Suggested beverage

Awamori  Yamakawa  Thailand rice  Yamakawa Sake Brewery (Okinawa Pref.)
泡盛  やまかわ  品種：タイ米  山川酒造（沖縄）

## SALMON

*Deep-fried salmon is topped with beautiful salmon caviar and mayonnaise. With a glass of dry rosé from Provence, the pleasantly salty flavor of the salmon and its caviar creates an exhilarating sensation.*

## サーモン

揚がったサーモンの上に、程よい塩味のイクラをトッピング。プロヴァンスの辛口のロゼワインと楽しむサーモンとイクラの塩気とマヨネーズの酸味が爽快に感じます。

### Suggested beverage

Rosé Wine  Chateau Baillon (Grenache 40% Cinsaut40% Syrah20%) (Otes de Provence)

ロゼワイン　シャトーサンバイヨン　品種：グルナッシュ・サンソー他　コート・ド・プロヴァンス

**STRING BEANS**
隠元豆

**POTATO**
馬鈴薯

# STRING BEANS

*Cheese snuggles with string beans in pork. A rather unusual combination of ingredients, but these three mingle well to create a superior taste. To complement this dish, fresh Junmai Ginjo made from finest rice is a must.*

# 隠元豆

チーズの周りを隠元豆で囲み豚肉で巻きました。意外な組み合わせですが、お互いが引き立て合う三位一体の味わい。フレッシュな純米吟醸との相性が絶妙。

## Suggested beverage

Sake Urakasumizen (Junmai Ginjo)  Yamadanishiki Toyonisiki   Saura Co,.Ltd., (Miyagi Pref.)

日本酒　浦霞禅（純米吟醸）　品種：山田錦　トヨニシキ　佐浦（宮城）

# POTATO

*The familiar ingredients of this dish-potato and smoked bacon-belie the exquisiteness of this kushinobo. Spicy red wine from New Zealand adds an extra touch to the flavor.*

# 馬鈴薯

親しみのある食材だけに串揚げの美味しさを確認出来る一品と言えるでしょう。ニュージーランドのスパイシーな赤ワインとベーコンのスモーク感を合わせました。

## Suggested beverage

Red Wine  GLADSTONE URLAR   Pino Noir   Nishi Sake Brewery (New Zealand)

赤ワイン　グラッドストーン　アーラー　品種：ピノ・ノワール　西酒造（ニュージーランド）

**SNOW CRAB MEAT**
蟹鱆巻

## SNOW CRAB MEAT

*Snow crab meat is plentiful in whiting rolls which are steam-fried. The tangy and mineral notes of Daiginjo merge with the flavor of the crab for a delightful taste.*

### 蟹鱚巻

ずわい蟹の身を贅沢に使い、鱚に巻いて蒸し揚げにしました。特に蟹に合う大吟醸のミネラル感は蟹の風味との絶妙のマリアージュでとても楽しめるものがあります。

### Suggested beverage

Sake Kokuryu-Shizuku (Dai ginjo)　Yamadanishiki　Kokuryu Sake Brewing (Fukui Pref.)

日本酒　黒龍しずく（大吟醸）　品種：山田錦　黒龍酒造（福井）

# MATSUTAKE MUSHROOM

The matsutake mushroom is deep-fried and a squeeze of sudachi, a small citrus fruit, is added to give an accent. Rich-flavored Japanese white wine blends well with the aroma and juicy texture of the mushroom.

# 松 茸

松茸をシンプルに揚げてスダチを。リッチな日本産の白ワインを合わせることにより、松茸の香ばしくてジューシーな食感と見事に調和します。

MATSUTAKE
松 茸

## Suggested beverage

White Wine   SAYS FARM CHARDONNAY   Chardonnay   T-MARKS Co.,Ltd., (Toyama Pref.)

白ワイン　セイズファーム・シャルドネ　品種：シャルドネ　T-MARKS（富山）

**DUCK WITH LEEK**
鴨葱

## DUCK WITH LEEK

*Duck and leek go ever so well together; this is a well-known fact in Japan. Their marriage is exhibited in this kushinobo recipe. The refined yet powerful character of Junmai-shu is a natural choice for this duck dish.*

## 鴨葱

鴨と葱は相性がいいことで有名。串揚げも鴨と葱の抜群の相性を遺憾なく発揮します。やはり鴨には、上品さと力強さを兼ねた純米酒を選びました。

### Suggested beverage

SAKE   Kamenoo Gaijin (Junmai)  Kamenoo   Maruo-honten (Kagawa Pref.)

日本酒　亀の尾　凱陣（純米）　品種:亀の尾　丸尾本店（香川）

**PRAWN**
車海老

## PRAWN

*Kurumaebi prawn is at its freshest when deep-fried. Enjoy its sweetness, including the pleasantly crisp head and tail. Top-quality refined sake will lift the flavour of this dish to impress you even more.*

### 車海老

車海老は活きたものをお揚げします。車海老の甘み、頭や尻尾の香ばしい食感など、持ち味の全てを堪能して下さい。純米の日本酒がさらに旨さを持ち上げます。

### Suggested beverage

Sake　Sawaya-Matsumoto (Junmai) Gohyakumangoku　Matsumoto Sake Brewery (Kyoto Pref.)

日本酒　澤屋まつもと（純米）　品種：五百万石　松本酒造（京都）

**WHITING WITH BACON**
鱚ベーコン

## WHITING WITH BACON

*Parsley sandwiched between celery pieces is wrapped in bacon and then rolled in whiting. Bite-size rolls fill your mouth with a cosmos of flavor. We recommend Loire white for its harmony with fish dishes.*

## 鱚ベーコン

セロリでパセリをはさみ、それをベーコンで巻き、さらに鱚で巻いています。一口でいただく味わいは小宇宙。ロワール地方の白ワインは魚との相性の良さで選びました。

### Suggested beverage

White Wine Sancerre (Sauvignon Blanc) Domaine Andre Nevue Et Fils (Loire)
白ワイン　サンセール　品種：ソーヴィニオンブラン　ドメーヌ・アンドレ・ヌヴ・エ・フィス（ロワール）

## CUTTLEFISH

*Celebrate the sweet duet of cuttlefish and sea urchin. White wine full of mineral highlights the taste of the cuttlefish, blending it with the exquisite flavor of the sea urchin.*

## 紋甲烏賊

紋甲烏賊と雲丹の甘みがハーモニーを奏でます。ミネラルたっぷりの白ワインが紋甲烏賊の甘みを打ち出す役目をしつつ雲丹の旨味にもマッチします。

**CUTTLEFISH**
紋甲烏賊

### Suggested beverage

White Wine  Muscadet (Sèvre et Maine Sur Lie)  Le "L"dor Pierre Luneau Papin (Loire)

白ワイン　ミュスカデ（セブレエメーヌ・シュールリー）　エルドール・ピエール・ルノー・パパン　（ロワール）

**ROLLED BURDOCK WITH CONGER EEL**
牛蒡穴子巻

**BITE-SIZED EGGPLANT**
小切茄子

# ROLLED BURDOCK WITH CONGER EEL

*Seasoned burdock is wrapped in conger eel and deep-fried on skewer. This kushinobo recipe blends the two into an attractive taste. Try it with potato spirit shochu made with Japanese pepper, preferably with soda.*

## 牛蒡穴子巻

味付けしていた牛蒡を穴子で巻きました。個性の強い組み合わせですが、串揚げにすると一体感が出て魅了が増します。芋焼酎にフレッシュな山椒を浸漬して更に蒸留した山椒芋焼酎で合わせました。炭酸割りで。

## Suggested beverage

Imo-Shochu  AKAYANE Sansho Spirit  Shoshu & Sansho  Satasouji-shouten (Kagoshima Pref.)

芋焼酎　アカヤネ山椒スピリッツ　佐多宗二商店 ( 鹿児島 )

# BITE-SIZED EGGPLANT

*A bite-sized eggplant is stuffed with a minced chicken-and-ginger mixture and topped with sweet miso paste. Have some brown-sugar shochu spirit on the rocks with the dish. The subtle sweetness of the shochu hamonizes will with the miso paste.*

## 小切茄子

小切茄子の中に鶏ミンチと生姜の練ったものを詰め、田楽味噌をトッピングしました。田楽味噌の甘みと、黒糖焼酎のほのかな甘みを合わせました。ロックで。

## Suggested beverage

Kokutou-Shochu  Ryugu (Brown Sugar)  Tomita Sake Brewery (Amami-ooshima. Kagoshima Pref.)

黒糖焼酎　龍宮　富田酒造場（鹿児島・奄美大島）

# PORK TENDERLOIN

## 豚 肉

*Filleted pork is skewered with leek. This traditional dish is one of the origins of kushinobo cooking. We have chosen Junmai Daiginjo to go with this pork dish.*

豚フィレ肉と長葱を刺しました。串揚げの伝統的なアイテムで、原点でもある一品です。ふくよかで力強い純米大吟醸を豚肉料理の相性の良さで選びました。

PORK TENDERLOIN
豚肉

## Suggested beverage

Sake   Gorin (Junmai Daiginjo)   Yamadanishiki   Syata Shuzou Co,Ltd. (Toyama Pref.)

日本酒　五凛（純米大吟醸）　品種：山田錦　車多酒造店（富山）

SCALLOP
帆立貝

## SCALLOP

*The delicate ocean scent of scallops is complemented by sweet vinegar. Light, pleasant Alsace white wine will enhance the wonderful taste of the scallops even more.*

## 帆立貝

ほんのりと潮のかおりがする帆立貝は甘酢によって引き立てられ、甘くて旨い一品です。軽やかに飲める、アルザスの白ワインは、帆立貝の甘さを引き立てます。

### Suggested beverage

White Wine　Riesling　Domaine Albert Boxler (Alsace)
白ワイン　リースリング　ドメーヌ・アルベール・ボクスレー（アルザス）

**RICE CAKE**
餅

## *RICE CAKE*

The combination of rice cake, spicy cod roe and seaweed is a unique Japanese food culture. The delicate taste of rice cake and the spicy flavor of the cod roe match well with the Junmai Daiginjo.

## 餅

餅と明太子と海苔の組み合わせは日本特有の食文化の一品です。餅の甘み、明太子の味わいがこの純米大吟醸に程よくマッチします。

### Suggested beverage

Sake Masuizumi Kotobuki Platinum Junmai Daiginjo　Yamadanishiki　Masuda Sake Brewery (Toyama Pref.)

日本酒　満寿泉　純米大吟醸　寿　プラチナ　品種：山田錦　桝田酒造店 (富山)

Spring

春

## BAMBOO SHOOT

*The aroma of freshly-picked bamboo shoot, minced chicken and spring in the air make a special trio. This dish is available only during the bamboo shoot season. Don't miss the chance to experience the wonderful flavour of Spring!*

### 筍

香りのいい筍を選び、鶏ミンチ、木の芽で、春を感じる三重奏。旬の生の筍が入荷する時季だけの提供になります。限られた期間だけ味わえる筍のおいしさを体験してください。

BAMBOO SHOOT

RAPE BLOSSOMS

菜の花

筍

# *RAPE BLOSSOMS*

*The young tips of field mustard offer you a fresh spring breeze of flavour. Rolled carefully in thinly sliced beef and flavoured with dashistock, they are a very sexy dish（we think!）.*

## 菜の花

やわらかい菜の花の新芽は春の息吹を感じさせてくれます。出汁で味付けされた菜の花と巻いている牛肉との相性は、官能的です。

**HALFBEAK**

**JAPANESE BUTTERBUR**

# HALFBEAK

*A fresh, delicate flavour, seasoned with honewort. The distinctive flavour of the plant spices the subtle taste of the fish just right.*

## 針魚

三つ葉を針魚（サヨリ）で巻いています。繊細な針魚の味わいを三つ葉の香りが引き立ててくれます。繊細で、さっぱりとした味わいです。

# JAPANESE BUTTERBUR

*Butterbur is flavoured with dashistock and carefully rolled in thin layers of deep-fried tofu. Butterbur is a vegetable unique to Japan that harmonizes perfectly with tofu. Why don't you experience its distinctive texture?*

## 蕗

*蕗（フキ）を出汁で味付けをして薄揚げで束ねて巻きました。蕗は日本特有の野菜です。歯触りに個性がありますので薄揚げとの食感もよく味わってください。*

蕗

針魚

# BROAD BEAN

*Taste the full flavour of broad beans. Boiled and skinned, they are rolled in thinly sliced sea bream. The bean's texture and the ocean taste of the sea bream blend perfectly.*

## 蚕豆

ホクホクの蚕豆（そらまめ）が味わえます。蚕豆は茹でて皮をむいて、鯛で巻きます。蚕豆の甘さと鯛の旨みで風味の豊かさが倍増し、相性の良さがわかります。

**BROAD BEAN**

**PIKE EEL**

鱧

蚕豆

## *PIKE EEL*

*The refreshing flavour of pike eel is well-suited to kushinobo. Following tradition, we serve it with a tart plum sauce. This combination is said to act as a pick-me-up in the heat of summer.*

### 鱧

あっさりした味わいの鱧（はも）は串揚げにもよく合います。やはり、梅肉ソースを合わせてみました。鱧と梅肉は定番の組み合わせですが、夏に元気が出る組み合わせでもあります。

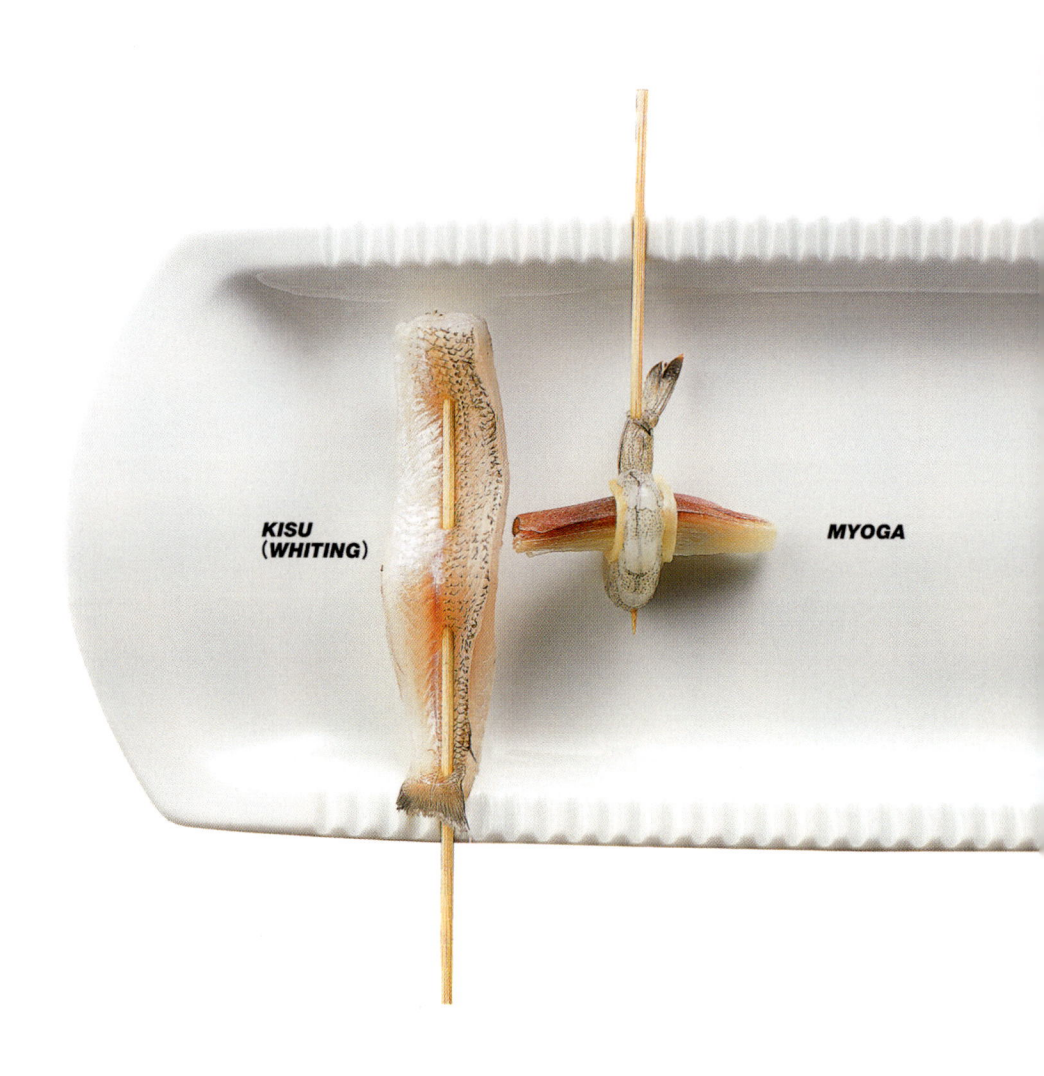

KISU
(WHITING)

MYOGA

## *KISU*(*WHITING*)

*Deep-fried kisu is soft and sweet enough to melt in the mouth. The topping of chopped onion, celery and parsley is a good match and leaves an enjoyable aftertaste.*

### 鱚

揚げたての鱚（キス）は、口の中でとろけるようなやわらかさで、甘みも広がります。玉葱やセロリやパセリのみじん切りのトッピングが鱚と良くマッチし、楽しい余韻も残してくれます。

茗 荷 　　　　　　　　　鱚

## *MYOGA*

*Japanese ginger wrapped in shiba shrimp and deep-fried. Many are surprised at how well ginger and shrimp complement each other. Enjoy the attractive appearance first, then the firm texture of the ginger, and finally the invigorating after-taste.*

## 茗 荷

茗荷（ミョウガ）を芝海老で巻いて揚げました。茗荷と海老の相性の良いことに驚かれる人も多いようです。見た目の楽しい形と、茗荷の歯触りとすがすがし後味を順番に楽しんで味わってください。

**CHESTNUT**

**GINKGO NUT**

# GINKGO NUT

*Ginkgo nuts embedded in slices of sausage and skewered for deep-frying. The lasting appeal of kushi-nobo cuisine lies in the enjoyment of such new tastes, born of careful preparation and creative ideas.*

## 銀 杏

銀杏はウインナーソーセージに埋め込んでから串に刺しました。こうした手間とアイデアから生まれる新しい味わいを楽しんでもらうのが、串揚げの食文化の奥深いところです。

Autumn
秋

# CHESTNUT

*Large chestnuts wrapped in slices of chicken tenderloin.  The individual tastes of chestnuts and chicken combine in a rich flavour that fills the mouth.*

## 栗

大粒の栗です。栗は鶏ささ身を巻きました。熱いうちに召し上がって、鶏肉と栗の味わいを噛みしめてみてください。栗だけ、鶏肉だけより一緒のほうが味の厚みがグンと広がります。

銀杏

栗

# SWEET POTATO

*Sweet potato, steamed and strained, combined with black sesame.  Straining makes the sweet potato melt in your mouth.  Its natural sweetness won't spoil the flavor of your sake.*

## 薩摩芋

薩摩芋は蒸して裏ごしして黒胡麻と合わせました。裏ごししてあるので、口溶けがよく食べやすいので、まさに串揚げ版スウィートポテトです。

**SAKURA SHRIMP**

**SWEET POTATO**

薩摩芋

桜海老

## *SAKURA SHRIMP*

*Stardust shrimp, fished from November onwards, has a taste all its own. Wrapping it in yuba (bean curd sheet) before it is deep-fried enhances its fragrance.*

### 桜海老

11月に解禁になる秋漁の桜海老はまた格別のおいしさがあります。湯葉で包んで揚げますから、桜海老そのものの香ばしさ、甘さの広がりを味わえます。

Autumn

秋

# MONKFISH

*Meaty monkfish is a hearty winter dish. Deep-frying brings out its full flavour and lemony ponzu adds a little kick.*

## 鮟鱇

鮟鱇（あんこう）の弾力のある身は冬のごちそうです。ポン酢おろしをアクセントでのせてお出しします。鮟鱇は淡白な魚ですが、揚げ物にしたときに味わい深く、ポン酢によってさっぱりと仕上ります。

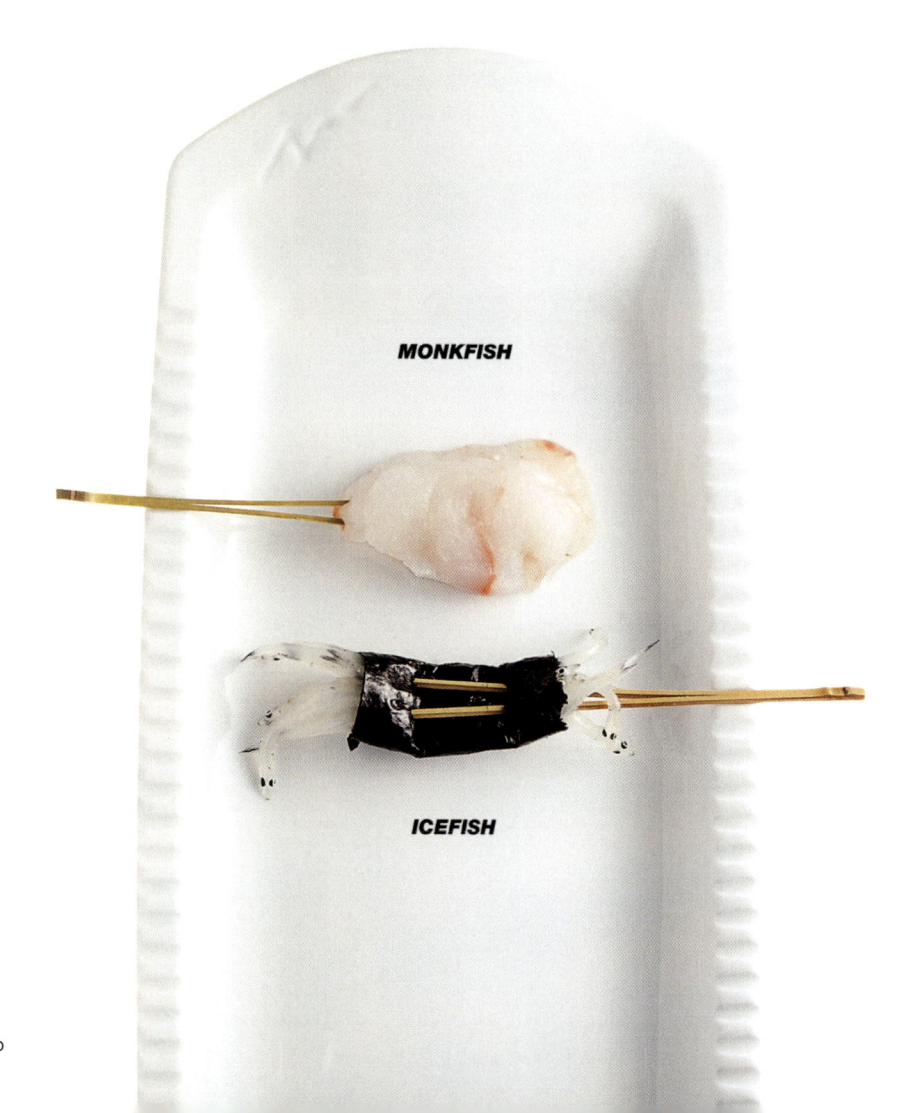

**MONKFISH**

**ICEFISH**

白 魚

鮟鱇

# *ICEFISH*

*Icefish (Shirauo) wrapped in nori and deep-fried. Savor a classic winter delicacy as the aroma of the seashore fills your mouth.*

## 白 魚

白魚は海苔で巻いて揚げます。口の中で広がる磯の香りとともに冬ならではの味覚を味わってください。

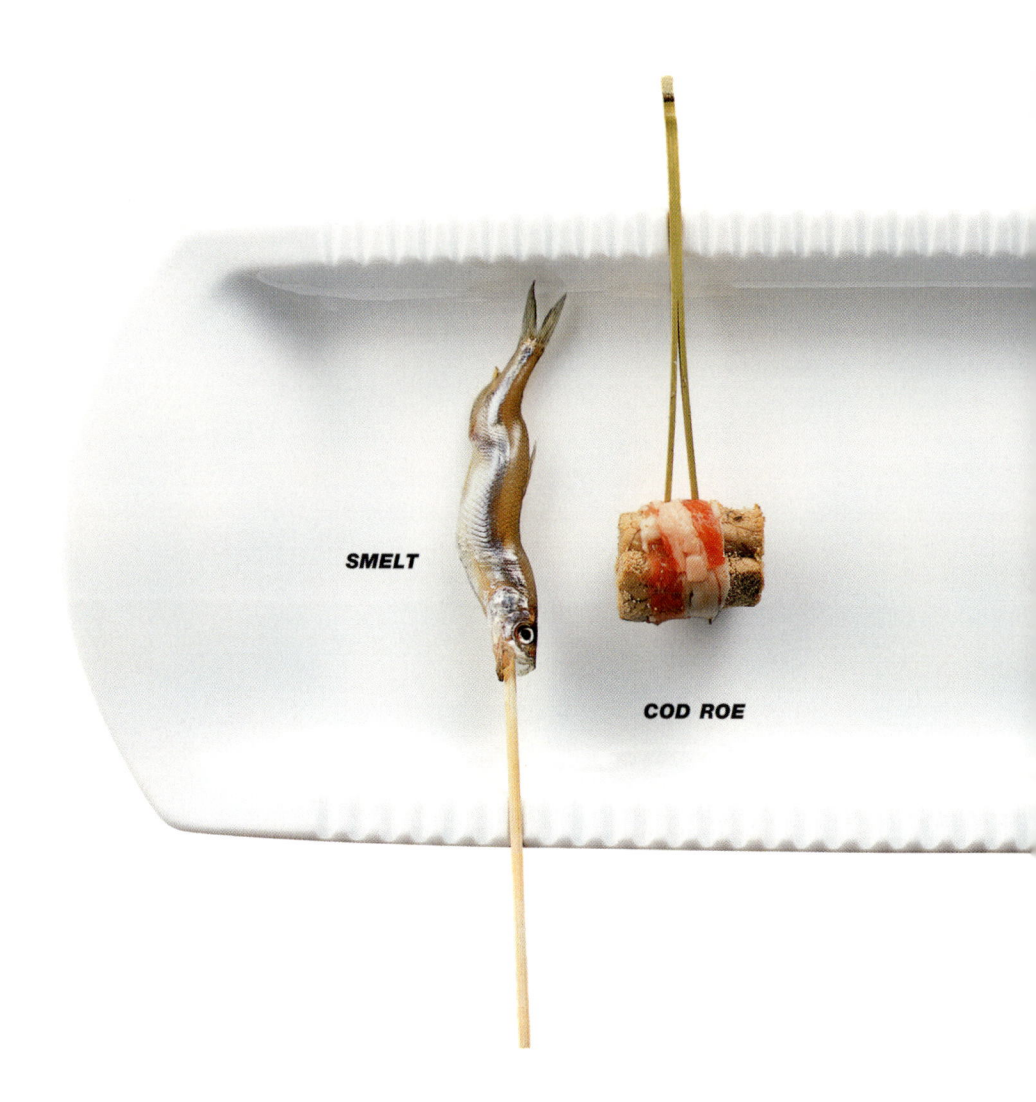

SMELT

COD ROE

## *COD ROE*

*Cod roe and thinly sliced pork may sound like a peculiar combination but they make a perfect match.  This is a very popular winter kushinobo.  Take our word for it.*

## 鱈子

鱈子（タラコ）は淡く味付けして炊いたものです。これに豚バラ肉を巻きました。珍しい組み合わせと思うでしょうが、相性は抜群です。冬の人気アイテムです。

鱈子

公魚

## *SMELT*

*Bite-size smelt are individually deep-fried on skewers. Enjoy the crunchy breading and the fluffy flesh and pleasantly crisp edible bones of smelt, not to mention its wonderful aroma.*

## 公魚

ひと口で食べられる公魚（ワカサギ）を一尾串に刺しました。ふっくらと揚がった公魚は小骨がありますが、とても香ばしくておいしく召し上がれます。

# kushinobo's side-dishes

### *OBUZUKE*
*おぶづけ*

After your kushinobo, try some rice in "obuzuke" style. Our rice is grown in Fukushima with tender care by Mr. Toshihiko Ito. Top it with our original sesame salt and some "shiofuki" kombu (from Osaka by Oguraya), and complete it by pouring "obu" (green tea, in the kansai region dialect) over it.

串揚げの後にはおぶづけを、どうぞ。「おぶ」とは関西弁でお茶のこと。お米は福島の伊藤俊彦さんが丹誠込めて作った米。昆布は大阪小倉屋の汐冨貴。胡麻岩塩は自家製のものです。

# Cheese

At our Kushinobo 1950 restaurant, several varieties of cheese are offered to customers at 10 o'clock most evenings,. The cheeses are made exclusively from the milk of 16 cows who are looked after with tender care by Mr. and Mrs. Yoshida at Yoshida Farm in Okayama, Japan. Kushinobo 1950's cheese is served with the hope that the excellence of Japanese cheese become known to the rest of the world.

「kushinobo」では毎夜10時になると、岡山の吉田牧場・吉田全作夫妻が丹誠込めて育てている十六頭の牛から採る牛乳のみで作るチーズが楽しめる。このチーズを通じて世界の人々に日本産チーズの素晴らしさを伝えたい。

**❶ camembert**
カマンベール

**❷ ricotta**
リコッタ

**❸ fontina**
フォンティーナ

**❹ caciocavallo**
カッチョカバロ

**❺ fresh cheese**
フレッシュチーズ

**❻ mozzarella**
モツァレラ

### cheese time

It's 10 p.m., cheese time! Kushinobo 1950 is the place not only for delicious deep-fried skewered food but also for a good time with cheese and drinks. Cheese time begins with the ever-popular cheek-to-cheek dance tune "Mary Jane," by Hiro ☆ Tsunoda. ("cheese" to "cheek" – just a play on words – get it? Don't start dancing, though!)

週末には朝5時まで営業している「kushinobo」では毎夜10時になると「チーズタイム」に。もちろん串揚げも楽しめるが、チーズとお酒を楽しむだけの利用もできる。「チーズタイム」が始まる合図はつのだ☆ひろ氏のチークタイムの定番曲「メリー・ジェーン」。「チーク」と「チーズ」をかけた洒落だ。間違えて踊らないように…。

# Let's cook kushinobo

## *POTATOES*

[馬鈴薯]の作り方

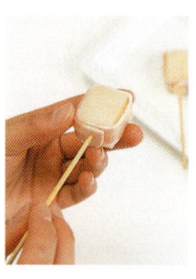

Steam and peel potatoes and cut into bite-size pieces. Season lightly with salt and pepper and wrap in bacon.

ジャガイモは蒸して皮をむき、食べやすい大きさに切ります。軽く塩・胡椒をしてベーコンを巻きます。

Pierce with the skewer, making sure that the point does not emerge, as this would make them dangerous to eat. (This is true of all kushinobo.)

串は先が突き出ないように刺します。食べるときに危ないからです。全ての串揚げも同様に。

# ROLLED SHRIMP WITH SHISO LEAVES

## [芝海老紫蘇巻]の作り方

1. Place the back of the shiso leaf on your palm with the point toward you, and lay the shrimp in the middle of it.

大葉の裏側を手のひらにひろげ、その中央に海老を置きます。

2. Fold the point of the leaf away from you, over the shrimp.

葉の先のほうを折って海老を挟みます。

3. Fold the top left of the shiso leaf toward you to enclose the shrimp.

大葉の左上を手前に折って海老を包みます。

4. Fold the top right of the shiso leaf toward you to enclose the shrimp.

次に大葉の右上を手前に折って海老を包みます。

5. Roll the shrimp away from you to wrap it neatly in the shiso leaf.

海老を向こう側に回転させて大葉がぴったり巻きつくようにします。

6. Insert the skewer through two wrapped shrimps one after the other, as shown.

大葉で巻いた海老2尾を並べて串に刺します。

# *LOTUS ROOT*

## ［蓮根］の作り方

Peel the lotus root, then cut into slices about ⅕in.(5mm) thick. Match the shapes and number holes of the slices to these illustrations (the ideal number of holes is three).

蓮根は皮をむいて５ミリ厚ほどの輪切りにして形、穴の数を揃えます。穴３個がベスト。

Fill the lotus root holes with minced beef mixed with curry powder, then insert the skewer into the end of the slice and pierce it lengthwise.

蓮根の穴にカレー粉を混ぜた牛挽き肉を詰め、串に刺します。

# ASPARAGUS AND SLICED PORK

［アスパラ］の作り方

Cut bacon or belly pork in strips approximately ⅛. (2mm) thick, ⁵/₈ in. (15mm) wide, and 12in. (30cm) long. wrap asparagus spirally, from the tip to 6in. (15cm) from the large end.

豚バラ肉は巻きやすいように幅を約１５ミリくらいに切っておき、先のほうから巻いていく。

# STUFFED CHICKEN WING

## [手羽先]の作り方

1　Remove the tips of the chicken wings with a carving knife.

手羽先の先端を包丁で切り落とします。

5　Tenderize meat by pounding it with heel of the sharp side of a knife and remove any tendons. The meat is ready for cooking.

包丁で肉を叩いて、筋を切って火が通りやすくしておきます。

2　Open up the chicken wings with the carving knife, and remove the thinner bone.

手羽先を包丁で開いて、細いほうの骨を取り出します。

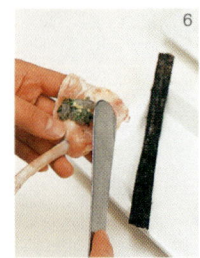

6　Place minced shrimp mixed with chopped shiso on the chicken meat.

鶏肉の部分に大葉を混ぜた海老ミンチをのせます。

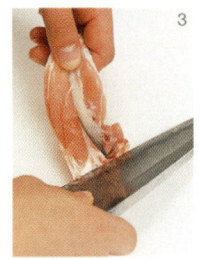

3　Cut off the joint parts of the chicken wings with the carving knife, and separate the meat from the bone.

手羽先の関節部分を包丁でしごいて、骨と肉を切り離します。

7　Rotate the wing bone so that the minced shrimp is wrapped in the chicken.

手羽の骨を回転させて、のせた海老ミンチを鶏肉で巻いた状態にします。

4　Lift up the separated joint bone, and level the meat to an equal thickness by scraping with the edge of the carving knife.

切り離した関節部分の骨を持ち上げ、肉を包丁の歯でならして均等の厚みにします。

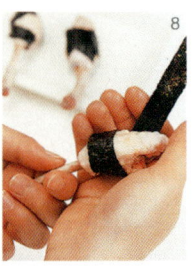

8　Wrap in nori cut about 7/8 in. (2cm) wide while rotating the wing bone as above, to complete the dish.

1センチ幅に切った海苔を同じく手羽の骨を回転させながら巻き付けて完成です。

# SALMON

[鮭]の作り方

1　Cut the salmon to a rectangle as shown and lightly season one side with salt and pepper.

形を揃えて切ったサーモンは片面に軽く塩・胡椒を振ります。

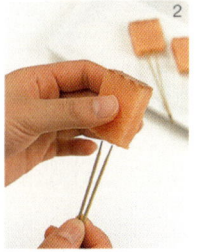

2　Turn the skin side of the salmon upwards, and pierce lengthwise from one end with the skewer.

サーモンは、皮目を上にし、串は下から上に向かって刺します。

# STRING BEANS

[隠元豆]の作り方

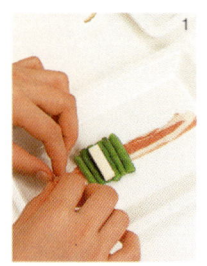

Cut parboiled string beans into three equal pieces. Pack six pieces around a strip of cheese of similar size. Place these on a ⅛in × 1in × 4in (2mm × 2.5cm × 10cm) strip of bacon or belly pork.

さっと茹でた隠元豆を三等分に切ります。豚バラ肉の上にチーズと隠元豆を置きます。

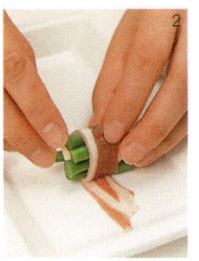

Wrap the pork so that the cheese is in the middle with the beans around it, and insert the split skewer as shown.

チーズが中心で、その周りに隠元豆がくるように豚肉で巻いて、串に刺します。

# PORK TENDERLOIN

[豚肉]の作り方

Cut pork fillet and onion to cubes of about the same size. Lightly sprinkle the pork with salt and pepper.

豚ヒレ肉と玉ねぎは同じくらいの大きさに切ります。豚肉には軽く塩・胡椒を振ります。

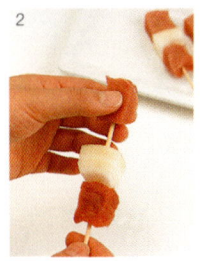

Insert the skewer so that pork is on each side of the onion.

豚肉の間に玉ねぎがくるように串に刺します。

# ROLLED BURDOCK WITH CONGER EEL

## ［牛蒡穴子巻］の作り方

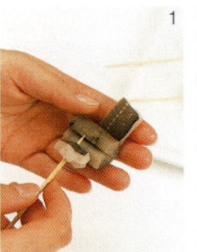

1 Simmer burdock for 15min. in dashistock and add soy sauce to taste. Cut in 1½in(4cm) pieces. Place a piece on the skin side of a strip of conger eel, and pierce the flesh side of the eel with the skewer.

炊いて味付けした牛蒡を、穴子の皮側にのせ、その裏から串を刺します。

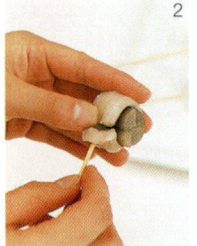

2 Roll the conger eel towards you to wrap the burdock.

穴子を手前に向かって丸めて牛蒡を巻きます。

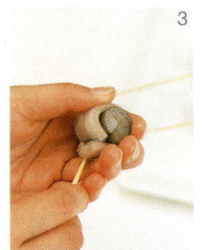

3 Push the skewer through the end of the rolled conger eel, also skewering the burdock.

巻いた穴子の端に串を通し、突き刺して牛蒡にも串を通します。

# ROLLED CELERY WITH WHITING AND BACON

## ［鱚ベーコン］の作り方

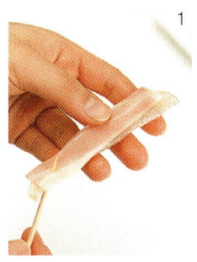

1 Debone whiting. Cut in strips 3/4 in × 5 in (2cm × 12cm). Cut bacon to about the same size and lay it on the skin side of the whiting. Pass the skewer through the whiting first.

鱚の皮目側に同じくらいの大きさに切ったベーコンを重ねます。鱚のほうから串を刺します。

2 Place parsley sandwiched by celery on the bacon.

ベーコンの上にパセリを挟んだセロリを置きます。

3 Roll the whiting and bacon towards you and wrap the celery.

鱚とベーコンを手前に向かって丸めてセロリを巻きます。

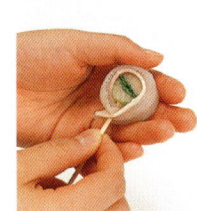

4 Pass the skewer through the end of the rolled whiting, also skewering the celery.

鱚の端に串を通し、突き刺してセロリにも串を通します。

# BREADING

## BATTER
[ネリヤ]の作り方

| | |
|---|---|
| 6 eggs | 卵…6 個 |
| 250ml milk | 牛乳…250ml |
| 300~350g flour | 小麦粉…300～350g |
| a little salt | 塩…少々 |
| 15ml sake | 日本酒…15ml |
| 5g sugar | 砂糖…5g |

## BREADCRUMBS
[パン粉]

Use fine breadcrumbs. If coarse, refine them in a mixer.

パン粉は細かいものがベストです。粗いものならば、ミキサーにかけて細かくします。

## DREDGING
衣のつけ方

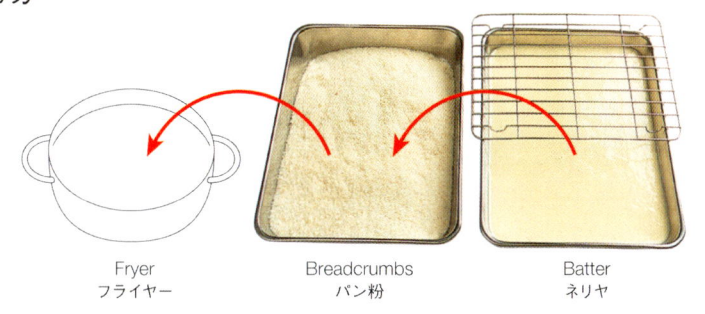

Fryer
フライヤー

Breadcrumbs
パン粉

Batter
ネリヤ

Set the breadcrumbs near the fryer for good deep-frying.
上手に揚げるためにフライヤーの近くにパン粉を置こう。

1 Mix the ingredients for the batter slowly, to prevent it from becoming pasty. Pass the skewered item through the batter.

ネリヤの材料は、ねばりが出ないようにゆっくり混ぜ、串に刺した材料をくぐらせます。

The batter should be soft enough for "threads" to hang down. After passing skewered item through the batter, put it down momentarily to remove the threads.

ネリヤは糸を引いてたれるやわらかさで。材料をくぐらせたら少しだけ置いて落します。

3 Place the skewered item coated with batter in the breadcrumbs.

パン粉にネリヤを付けた材料をのせます。

4 Sprinkle breadcrumbs on top of kushinobo. Do not press down on the breadcrumbs from above.

上からパン粉をかぶせます。このときパン粉の上から押さえないこと。

5 Cover evenly with breadcrumbs.

全体に均等にパン粉がつくようにまぶします。

6 Once the kushinobo has been breaded, put it in the oil witout delay!The oil temperature should be 350˚F(175˚C).

衣をつけたらすぐ揚げよう！

# KUSHINOBO SAUCE

## [串揚げソース]の作り方

| Stock | スープ |
|---|---|
| Fish bones | 魚のアラ |
| Chicken-wing bones | 手羽先の骨 |
| Shrimp shells | 芝海老の頭 |
| Vegetable Scraps | キャベツの芯 |
| Green onions | ネギの青葉 |
| Carrots | 人参 |
| Apples | リンゴ |
| Onions | 玉葱 |
| Eggshells | 卵の殻 |

| Recipe | レシピ |
|---|---|
| 750ml stock | スープ…750ml |
| 50g ketchup | ケチャップ…50g |
| 750ml Worcestershire sauce | イカリウスターソース…750ml |
| (IKARI, if available) | イカリとんかつソース…250ml |
| 250ml Tonkatsu sauce | 胡椒…小さじ1/2 |
| (IKARI, if available) | カレー粉…小さじ1/2 |
| 2~3g white pepper | 粉山椒…少々 |
| 2~3g curry powder | 生姜汁…少々 |
| A little Japanese pepper | にんにく汁…少々 |
| A little ginger-juice | 小麦粉…適量 |
| A little garlic-juice | |
| A little flour | |

1. Make a stock from fish bones, chicken bones and vegetable scraps.

魚のアラや手羽先の骨や野菜くずでスープをとります。

Add Worcestershire sauce, Tonkatsu sauce and seasoning, and heat over a medium flame to prevent burning.

スープとウスターソース、とんかつソース、調味料を加え、焦がさないように中火で炊きます。

Bring to the boil, then simmer for about 3 hours on the lowest flame (to prevent burning). Flour may be added to thicken while simmering.

沸いたら弱火にして焦がさないように約3時間炊きます。途中で小麦粉を加えてとろみをつけてもよいです。

# *SESAME SALT*

## [*胡麻岩塩*]の作り方

Toast the sesame, then grind coarsely in a mortar.

胡麻は炒ってから、すり鉢であらく当たります。

Add approximately the same amount of salt to the sesame.

胡麻とほぼ同量の塩を合わせます。

Add a little kobucha (powdered kombu with salt).

こぶ茶を少々加えます。

Mix all the ingredients to complete.

全体をよく混ぜてできあがり。

# Original goods in Kushinob

Sauces, ponzu, sesame salt, mustard and tomato ketchup are all neatly accommodated in one unit, there on the table ready to use. A stylish and functional design.

ソース、ポン酢、胡麻岩塩、マスタード、ケチャップ入れを一体化できるようにデザイン。常にテーブルの上にセットしてあるものだけに機能性とデザイン性の両方が求められる器だ。

**sauce & seasoning server**
ソース＆調味料入れ

**design by Hideyuki Matsuzaki**
松崎英之

To use the limited space on table and counter, Hideyuki Matsuzaki of MIYAMA redesigned the Kushinobo tableware to make it more compact, functional, and conceptually appropriate.

MIYAMAの松崎氏はテーブルやカウンターのスペースを有効に使えるように、機能的でコンパクト且つコンセプチュアルにリデザインした。

## beverage warmer (made of tin)
錫徳利（日本酒）、錫チロリ（焼酎）

Sake, shochu and water are warmed in traditional tin warmers. When shochu and water are gently warmed, they develop a wonderful mildness.

日本酒の燗と焼酎のお湯割りは、錫製のオリジナル酒燗器で提供。特に焼酎は水で割った焼酎全体をやさしく温めるので、口当たりが非常によい。

## vessel for obuzuke
おぶづけの器

Tea/snack set. A stylish set of teacup and snack bowl, for kombu seaweed, sesame salt and rice crackers.

おぶづけのセット。お茶を入れる器（写真右）と汐昆布や胡麻岩塩、あられを入れる器をお洒落に揃えている。

**❶ *vegetable stand***
野菜立て

**❷ *haze (goby)***
ハゼ

**❸ *kushinobo dish***
串揚げ皿

**❹ *kushinobo sauce dish***
ソース皿

**haze**
**串入れ**

Haze (goby) is a fish with a wide mouth.
Place finished skewers in this container that resembles a Haze with wide-open mouth.

「ハゼ」とは魚のハゼのこと。大きな口を開ける、その姿をモチーフにしたデザインで、食べ終わった串を入れる器だ。

## chinese tea set
### 中国茶道具

Chinese tea goes well with *kushinobo* dishes and even better in this Chinese tea set, comprising a teapot with stylish see-through design, an egg-timer for checking brewing time and a cup that enhances the tea's aroma and taste.

串揚げと相性のいい中国茶を楽しむ道具。茶葉の開き具合が見えるガラス製急須、香りを楽しみ味わう器、砂時計。

# 六本木 浜藤

## ふぐ料理の新しい世界

# Roppongi Hamato The New World of Fugu Cuisine

The year 2019 marks our 35th anniversary of Roppongi Hamato.
We have been expanding the new and fascinating world of fugu. "Roppongi Hamato"
has become the foundation of Kushinobo Co., Ltd. along with "Kushinobo"

2019年で創業35年を迎える『六本木 浜藤』。世界に通じるふぐ料理の新しい魅力を
開拓しました。串揚げの『串の坊』とともに、串の坊グループの両輪となっています。

# The Birth of Fugu + White Truffles + Caviar

## ふぐ＋白トリュフ＋キャビアの誕生

After meeting Satoshi Kimijima in 1998, we decided to improve the lineup of sake, shochu, and wines at our restaurants. When we traveled to Europe and visited wineries together, I realized many European people are intrigued by fugu (blowfish). However, majority of our foreign guests at our restaurants don't like ponzu sauce (soy sauce with citrus juice), a basic sauce for fugu.

There I thought, why not serve fugu with olive oil, white truffles, and salt for our foreign guests? In 2002, I was trying out new porridge with shirako (soft fugu roe) and porridge made from uncooked rice, just like risotto. I was just playing around with new ideas, and there I decided to add white truffles to fugu porridge. Its new and profound delicacy struck me like a lightning. In November of the following year 2003, we served "Fugu and White Truffles" for a limited time of three weeks, 50 guests per week, at our Roppongi Hamato. That was the beginning of this dish.

In 2004, a celebrity wrote a blog about this "Fugu and White Truffles". It was also covered on newspapers and magazines which dramatically increased our guests. We added an option to serve caviar in lieu of salt. When white truffles season passed around January, we started providing "Fugu and Black Truffles".

Fugu is one of the exceptional ingredients of Japan. What allowed me to match it with truffles and caviar, the exceptional ingredients of the world, was my sincere attitude towards the food and ingredients around the world. The result can be seen in Kushinobo Special (Page15). Fugu restaurant and Kushinobo restaurant have entirely different concepts, however, my aspiration to produce the best dish is the foundation I share for both venues.

君嶋哲至さんとの出会いで、お店に置く日本酒、焼酎、ワインを充実させ出したのが1998年からです。ワインの産地も君嶋哲至さんと一緒に巡るようになりました。そこで自己紹介をすると、欧州の人たちは、ふぐにすごく興味を示します。でも、日本で食べに来る外国のお客様はポン酢が苦手な人が多いのです。

そこで、ふぐをオリーブオイル、白トリュフ、塩で味わってもらったら外国の人に広く喜んでもらえるのではと考えたのです。2002年、白子雑炊とか、生米から炊く雑炊など、いろいろな雑炊に凝っていたこともあり、ふぐの雑炊に白トリュフを合わせてみました。お遊びのつもりでやったのですが、その深い味わい、初めての味は、脳裏に突き刺さりました。それで翌2003年11月に3週間だけ、一週間50名限定で『六本木 浜藤』で出したのが「ふぐと白トリュフ」の始まりです。

2004年には、有名人がブログで「ふぐと白トリュフ」を紹介してくれたり、新聞・週刊誌でも紹介され、客数は急増。塩の代わりにキャビアを合わせるバージョンも加えました。白トリュフの時季が過ぎた1月以降は「ふぐと黒トリュフ」も出すようになりました。

ふぐは、日本の最高の食材です。それにトリュフ、キャビアという世界で最高の食材を合わせることができたのは、世界中を旅して出会った様々な食材と、真摯に向き合ってきたからだと思います。その成果は「串の坊Special」（15ページ）にも反映されています。ふぐ店と串揚げ店——まったく別の業種ですが、最高の食事を目指すという点で、乾晴彦としての根幹は同じなのです。

## The Course of White Truffles, Wild-caught Tiger-fugu, Soft Fugu Roe & Caviar

*This menu is served only from the end of November to Christmas. The menu starts from appetizers to hot pot, with porridge as the final dish.*

## 白トリュフ、天然とらふぐ、白子＆キャビアのコース

*11月上旬からクリスマスまでのコースです。前菜から鍋、雑炊までの順に紹介します。*

**[Set Menu]**
コースの内容

❶ *Appetizer*
前菜

❷ *Steamed Egg Custard*
茶碗蒸し

❸ *Tessa (Fugu sashimi)*
てっさ

❹ *Grilled Soft Roe*
白子焼

❺ *Simmered Fugu Cutlet*
カツ煮

❻ *Hotpot*
てっちり

❼ *Porridge*
雑炊

### *Appetizer*
### 前菜

Jellied fugu topped with caviar and white truffles.

ふぐ白子を細かく切り、玉子、ふぐの煮凝りを添えてキャビアと白トリュフをトッピングしました。

### *Steamed Egg Custard*
### 白子茶碗蒸し

Steamed Egg Custard with white truffle topping.

白子茶碗蒸しの上に白トリュフをトッピングします。

### Tessa (Fugu Sashimi)
てっさ

Caviar on each piece of fugu sashimi, drizzled olive oil, topped with graded white truffles.

てっさ1枚ずつにキャビアをのせ、オリーブオイルをかけてから、白トリュフをおろしてかけます。

### Pan-seared
### 白子オリーブオイル焼

Fugu soft roe is seared with extra virgin olive oil and topped with white truffles.

白子をオリーブオイルでソテーして白トリュフをかけました。

### Grilled Soft Roe
### 白子岩塩焼

Optional menu available with caviar topping.

白トリュフと合わせてキャビアをトッピングするオーダーもできます。

### *Simmered Fugu Cutlet*
ふぐ白子カツ煮

Special menu available with fried soft
roe battered in egg.

裏メニューとしてふぐと白子をフライ
にしトリュフ玉子でとじるメニューも
あります。

# How to Enjoy White Truffles and Wild-caught Fugu Hotpot

## ［白トリュフ、天然とらふぐ鍋］の楽しみ方

Introducing how to eat hotpot and porridge, while enjoying the flavor of wild-caught fugu and the harmony it creates with the rich scent of white truffles.

鍋の食べ方から、雑炊まで、天然とらふぐならではの旨味と、白トリュフならでは
の芳醇な香味とのハーモニーを堪能できる楽しみ方を紹介します。

When the broth comes to a boil, put in fugu, maitake mushroom, and fugu skin. Fugu skin can only be taken from a fugu that is over 2kg.

だしが沸いたら、ふぐを入れ、舞茸とサメ皮を入れます。サメ皮は、2kg以上のふぐからしか取れない皮の部分です。

Add in the leeks, when the broth boils again, add in the Chinese cabbage.

続いて下仁田葱を入れ、だしが沸いたら白菜を半分入れます。

Grade some white truffles over the pot to add flavor and scent.

味付けとして白トリュフを鍋の上からマイクロカッターでおろしてかけます。

Take the simmered fugu, leek, and Chinese cabbage into your bowl, drizzle some olive oil, grade white truffles and enjoy.

煮えたふぐ、ねぎ、白菜を取り出し、オリーブオイルをかけて、来島海峡の藻塩と共に味わいます。

Put in the rest of the Chinese cabbage. When it's cooked, enjoy another round.

残りの白菜を鍋に入れて、煮えたら同様に、ふぐとねぎと白菜を取り出し、オリーブオイルと味わいます。

6 After fugu, leeks, and Chinese cabbage, put in the tofu. Take them out when warmed up, top with fugu skin, pour on soy sauce. Top that with some white truffles.

ふぐ、ねぎ、白菜を味わったら、豆腐（京都・とようけ屋）を入れます。豆腐は温まったら取り出し、上にサメ皮をのせ、醤油（金沢・直源醤油）をかけます。その上に白トリュフをかけて食べます。

7 Next up is the rice cake and shirataki (konnyaku noodles).

続いて餅。焼餅を入れて、白滝も入れます。

8 Lightly braise the crown daisy. Take it into your bowl with rice cake and shirataki, drizzle some olive oil and enjoy.

春菊はさっと火を通す程度で。春菊と餅と白滝を取り出して、来島海峡の藻塩と共に食べます。

# White Truffles, Fugu Porridge

## ［白トリュフふぐ雑炊］の作り方

**1** We don't add in the broth. The broth already has the condensed umami of fugu and vegetables so we take this perfectly concentrated broth to prepare the porridge. First, add salt and white truffles into the broth and enjoy the broth as a soup.

途中でだしは足しません。鍋にふぐや野菜の旨味が加わり、だしが詰まって、雑炊にしたときに最上の濃度になるように進行し、雑炊づくりにかかります。まずは、鍋のだしに来島海峡の藻塩と共にと白トリュフを合わせて、芳醇なだしそのものを味わっていただきます。

**2** Add in uncooked rice. This rice is preserved together with white truffles in an air-tight container to have the scent transferred.

生米を加えます。生米は白トリュフと一緒に密閉保存して白トリュフの香りを移したものを使います。その米を事前にふぐで取った出汁をに浸水しておきます。

**3** Stir everything together, cover the pot, and let it cook.

全体を混ぜて、蓋をして圧力をかけて炊きます。

Remove the lid, stir, cover it again. Make sure to skim the foam and stir occasionally to avoid letting it burn.

蓋を取って混ぜ、また蓋をして炊いて、アクを取りながら焦がさないようこまめに混ぜて炊いていきます。

Right before the rice is cooked, add in soft roe, stir lightly, turn off the heat, cover the pot and wait 3 minutes. For this white truffles porridge, we don't add in any eggs.

米が炊きあがる直前に白子を入れて、さっと混ぜて火を止め、蓋をして3分置きます。白トリュフの雑炊には玉子は入れません。

6

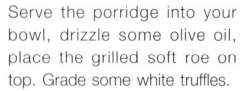

Serve the porridge into your bowl, drizzle some olive oil, place the grilled soft roe on top. Grade some white truffles.

雑炊を器に盛り、オリーブオイルをかけて焼いた白子をのせます。上から白トリュフをかけます。

7 We have an option to add caviar on the side.

さらにキャビア添えのご注文も受けます。

# The Set Menu of Black Truffles, Wild-caught Tiger-fugu, Soft Roe & Caviar

*We serve this menu at "Roppongi Hamato" from mid January to the end of mid March.*

## 黒トリュフ、天然とらふぐ、白子＆キャビアコース

黒トリュフのコースは、1月中旬から3月中旬までの『六本木浜藤』の
営業期間中にご提供します。

**［Set Menu］**
コースの内容

❶ **Appetizer**
前菜

❷ **Steamed Egg Custard**
茶碗蒸し

❸ **Tessa (Fugu sashimi)**
てっさ

❹ **Grilled Soft Roe**
白子焼

❺ **Simmered Fugu Cutlet**
カツ煮

❻ **Hotpot**
てっちり

❼ **Porridge**
雑炊

### Appetizer
### 前菜

Jellied fugu topped with caviar and black truffles.

ふぐ白子を細かく切り、玉子、ふぐの煮凝りを添えてキャビアと黒トリュフをトッピングしました。

### Steamed Egg Custard
### 茶碗蒸し

Steamed egg custard topped with black truffle.

茶碗蒸しに黒トリュフを入れました。

### *Tessa*
てっさ

Caviar on each piece of fugu sashimi, drizzle olive oil, topped with minced black truffles.

ひと切れずつのてっさにキャビアをのせ、オリーブオイルをかけて黒トリュフを刻んだものを散らしました。

### Fried Fugu
### ふぐ竜田揚げ

Fried fugu topped with black truffles.

ふぐの竜田揚げに黒トリュフをかけました。

### Grilled Soft Roe
### 白子焼

Caviar on grilled soft roe topped with minced black truffles.

白子焼にキャビアをのせ、黒トリュフを刻んだものをトッピングしました。

# How to Enjoy Black Truffles and Wild-caught Tora-fugu Hotpot

## ［黒トリュフ天然とらふぐ鍋］の楽しみ方

Introducing how to eat hotpot and porridge, a unique way to enjoy fugu hotpot.
You can taste the utmost flavor with the combination of fugu and black truffles.

鍋の食べ方から、雑炊まで、ふぐと黒トリュフの組み合わせだからこそ味わえる、
ふぐ鍋の新しい世界を紹介します。

**1** When the broth comes to a boil, put in fugu, maitake mushroom, and fugu skin.

だしが沸いたら、ふぐを入れ、舞茸とサメ皮を入れます。

**2** Add in the leeks, when the broth boils again, add the Chinese cabbage. Cook while skimming the foam occasionally.

続いて下仁田葱を入れ、だしが沸いたら白菜を半分入れます。アクを取りながら炊きます。味付けとして黒トリュフをマイクロカッターでおろしかけます。

**3** Take the simmered fugu, leeks, and Chinese cabbage into your bowl, drizzle some olive oil and enjoy.

煮えたふぐ、ねぎ、白菜を取り出し、EXV. オリーブオイルと塩をかけて味わいます。

**4** Add in the tofu. Take out when it's warm, top it with fugu skin, pour soy sauce and olive oil, top it with black truffles.

豆腐を入れ、豆腐が温まったら取り出し、サメ皮をのせ、醤油とオリーブオイルをかけ、黒トリュフをのせて食べます。

**5** Cook the rice cake. Crown daisy should be braised very lightly, eat it together with rice cake.

餅を入れて炊きます。春菊はさっと茹で、餅と一緒に食べます。

# *Black Truffles, Fugu Porridge*

## ［黒トリュフふぐ雑炊］の作り方

For black truffles porridge, we use cooked rice instead of uncooked rice. This rice is previously cooked in earthenware pot, then cooled to remove moisture.

黒トリュフの雑炊では、生米ではなくごはんを使います。土鍋で炊いて
冷蔵して水分を飛ばしたごはんで作ります。

1 First, enjoy the savory broth as a soup with only salt and black truffles.

まずは、鍋のだしに来島海峡の藻塩と黒トリュフを合わせて、芳醇なだしそのものを味わっていただきます。

2 We don't add in the broth. The broth already has the condensed umami of fugu and vegetables so we take this perfectly concentrated broth to prepare the porridge. Add in rice and stir.

だしは足しません。鍋にふぐや野菜の旨味が加わり、だしが詰まって、雑炊にしたときに最上の濃度になるようにして、雑炊づくりにかかります。土鍋で炊いた米をすぐに冷蔵庫で冷やし、水分を飛ばしたごはんを使います。

3 Stir occasionally to avoid burning, skim the foam. Add in soft roe, egg, turn off the heat and stir, cover with a lid and wait 3 minutes.

ごはんを焦がさないような混ぜながらアクも取って炊きます。白子を加えて混ぜ、卵を加えて火を止めて混ぜ、蓋をして3分置きます。

4 Stir the whole porridge and serve into your bowl. Drizzle olive oil and sprinkle minced black truffles.

全体を混ぜて器に盛り、オリーブオイルをかけて、黒トリュフを刻んでトッピングします。

# Kushinobo Roppongi Hills

Its luxurious interior is one of the notable features of Kushinobo Roppongi Hills. The 7.3-meter countertop is made from a single Japanese Cypress. Other tables are also made from the same cypress, providing a profound and calm composure. The artworks displayed in this restaurant including glass arts, Japanese lacquered tables, acrylic arts, diningware, and even the curtain holders are all made by renowned Japanese artists. With these artwork surroundings, you can enjoy an exceptional meal as if you are dining in a museum.

『串の坊　六本木ヒルズ店』は、贅を尽くしたインテリアが特徴。カウンターは7m30cmの檜の一枚板。その他のテーブルもすべて同じ檜で仕立てられ、重厚な存在感を放つ。店内随所に置かれたガラス細工、テーブルトップなどの漆、飾られたアクリルアート、使用する器、そして暖簾の留め木は、それぞれ日本を代表する作家によるもの。美術館さながらの名品に囲まれた店内で、非日常を感じつつ食事を楽しめる。

***Japanese Urushi Lacquer***
漆

### *YUI HIGASHIBATA*
### 東端 唯

Two hood pillars, the countertop, and table sides are designed with Japanese urushi lacquer by Yui Higashibata, a renowned urushi artist. Mixed together are colors of white, brown, and gold. White color is made from cashew-nuts-based material. The surface is processed with clear coating to give sturdiness and resilience against the dinnerware.

フードの2本の柱、カウンタートップ、テーブル横は漆でデザイン。漆芸家の第一人者、東端唯さんの作品。白・茶・金色の組み合わせ。漆で出せない白色は、カシューナッツの合成樹脂塗料で出した。表面にクリア加工をほどこして強度を高め、食器などをのせても大丈夫なようにしている。

## Glass
ガラス

### TAIZO YASUDA
安田泰三

In front of the counter is a lace-glass masterpiece by Taizo Yasuda. His artworks can be seen in various places inside the restaurant, all white to give a sense of unity. The light reflections that his artworks give off are artwork itself.

カウンター正面に安田泰三さんのレースガラス細工の大作が。店内各所にも安田さんの作品を。どれかが主張しないよう、白いものをセレクト。「こんなにたくさん置くの」と安田さんは驚いたそうだが、レースガラスが素敵に輝くライティングにたいへん満足している。

**Sculpture**
彫刻

### TSUTOMU IWASAKI
岩﨑 努

Curtain at the entrance called noren is usually supported by a piece of wood, but the large noren here is not held by an ordinary piece of wood. It is designed and made by a renowned Japanese sculptor Tsutomu Iwasaki. Iwasaki had never sculpted a noren holder before, however, after learning Yasumichi Morita was the main designer, whom he was a big fan of, he happily said yes to his request. With fire as its theme, it is a piece of art that captures your eyes and looks as if it will bewitchingly start moving.

ひときわ目立つ大きな暖簾。その暖簾の留め木（暖簾受け）は日本を代表する彫刻作家・岩﨑努氏の作品。暖簾の留め木は初めてのオーダーだったが、同店を設計した建築家の森田恭通氏のファンだったので、岩﨑氏は喜んで引き受けたという。「炎」をテーマにした、妖艶に動き出すかのような目を引き付ける暖簾の留め木だ。

**Sculpture of pershimmon is made by Tsutomu Iwasaki.**
柿の彫刻は、岩﨑努作

### *GAKU SHAKUNAGA*
釋永 岳

Dinnerware is crafted by ceramic artist Gaku Shakunaga. Shakunaga also has been a fan of Morita's works. Creating plates that do not interfere with the restaurant's atmosphere while considering their usability in a restaurant, Shakunaga experimented countless times and at last created pieces that define his essence.

器は、陶芸作家・釋永　岳氏によるもの。釋永氏も、同店を設計した森田恭通のファンだったという。スペシャルな空間を邪魔しないよう、また、飲食店の器として扱いやすさも考慮して何度も試作をし、釋永氏らしい器を完成させた。

**Acrylic Art**
アクリルアート

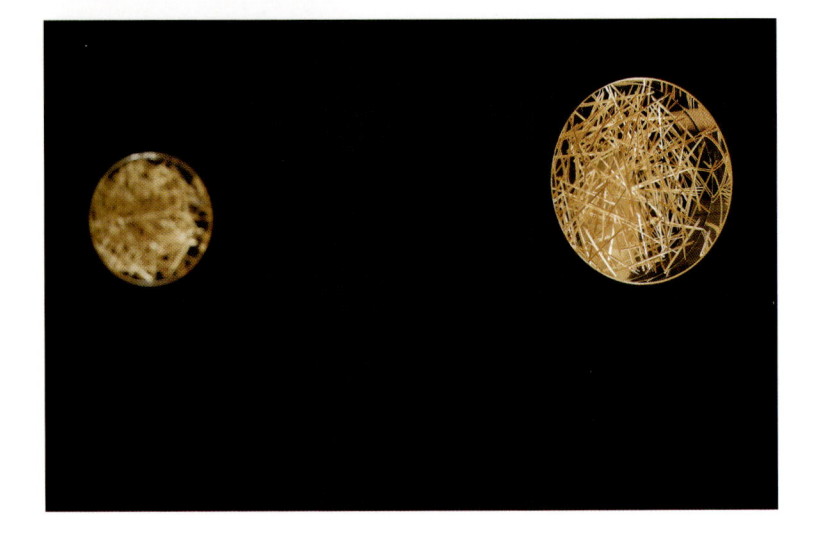

### TSUYOSHI YAMAMOTO
山本 剛

The artwork with skewers is a creation by an acrylic artist, Tsuyoshi Yamamoto. He created the three-dimensional look by repeating the process of pouring 10mm of acryl, and placing a skewer. He originally planned to use 100 skewers but right before completion, he decided to go with 108 skewers, a symbolic number that defines the number of human desires as stated in Buddhism teaching. He created six pieces in total and says it's miraculous that all came out with no damages.

店内に飾られた串を使ったオブジェは、アクリルアート第一人者の山本　剛氏の作品。アクリルを 10 ミリ流して串を置いて、アクリルを流して串をずらして置いて、の繰り返しで立体感を。100 本くらいを想定していたが、煩悩の数 (108 本 ) にしようと、完成間際に決めたそうだ。6 個作り、6 個とも割れたり変色しないで完成できたのは、奇跡的だという。

### Countertop Made From Single Japanese Cypress
檜の一枚板のカウンター

Countertop is made from a single Japanese Cypress, its length at 7.30m. This cypress was given by President Masuda from Masuda Sake Company.

カウンターは、檜の一枚板。仕上がりで7メートル30センチ。桝田酒造店の桝田社長が用意してくれた檜で作った。

### Iwase, Toyama
富山市の岩瀬エリア

Iwase is a port town in Toyama prefecture where buildings from early Edo era are still intact, maintaining the Edo atmosphere. Iwasaki, Shakunaga, and Yasuda each have their own studio in this town. Masuda Sake Company which produces Toyama's famous "Masuizumi" is also located in this area. Many artists from various fields are gathered around this town, and Iwase has now become a cultural origin.

彫刻家の岩﨑　努氏、陶芸家の釋永　岳氏、ガラス工芸作家の安田泰三氏がアトリエを構える富山市の岩瀬エリアは、江戸時代初期の建物が現存する港町で、当時の雰囲気を残している。富山の銘酒「満寿泉」の蔵元の桝田酒造店もここにある。現在は、様々な分野の作家がアトリエを構え、日本文化の発信地にもなっている。

# Roppongi Hamato

While many fugu restaurants tend to have zashiki-style seats or counters, the idea here was to give a French taste, where people dress up and dine. To give a casual touch, fugu motifs are hidden in the interiors, providing conversation topics.

ふぐ店は、お座敷やカウンターのイメージが強かったので、フレンチにドレスアップして行くような利用ができる店を追求したという。一方で、ところどころに、「ここにもふぐが」という仕掛けをほどこし、話題作りと気軽さを演出した。

This restaurant was fully renovated in 2009 for its 30th anniversary, designed by Yasumichi Morita.

2009 年の 30 周年のときに全面改装。デザインは森田恭通氏。

Partitions provide spaces similar to private rooms while you can enjoy the openness at the same time. Ceramic artworks made from fugu bones are displayed on the partitions. You may find a shirako-shaped piece if you look closely.

個室に近い間仕切りにして解放感を出した。間仕切りの上には、ふぐの骨を混ぜて焼いた磁器のアートワーク。よく見ると白子の形のものもある。

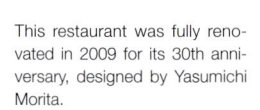

Lighting is made in an image of Tessa (fugu sashimi dish) plate.

てっさの皿をモチーフにした照明。

Fugu lantern is used as a rotating object.

ふぐちょうちんは、回転オブジェとして利用。

Cassina board is used to dry the fin in the process to make fugu fin sake.

ヒレ酒用のヒレを干す板はカッシーナで。

# The Birth Story

**How "Kushinobo Roppongi Hills" Was Born**

新生『串の坊　六本木ヒルズ店』の誕生物語

## The story behind the symbolic glass art

**Inui** "Kushinobo Roppongi Hills" was renewed in September 2018. Because we changed the location, I can say it was more of a new open rather than just a renewal. Opening a new restaurant requires a lot more investment which I had to consider carefully.

At that time, I visited Iwase-cho in Toyama Prefecture and saw Yasuda-san's glass art which is currently displayed in the restaurant, a powerful piece of art that weighs over 15kg. He said that was his last artwork of that size; he said it was physically demanding. I saw this piece of art and felt that I must display this in my restaurant, inspiring me to go ahead with the renovation. I had been planning to ask Morita-san for the interior design, so I had him see Yasuda-san's artwork.

**Morita** Yes, Inui-san and I went to

## 力をもらったガラス細工を店の象徴に

乾　2018年の9月に、『串の坊』の六本木ヒルズ店を全面リニューアルしました。場所も変わったので、リニューアルというより新規オープンですね。実は、新規オープンだと投資額も大きいですし、どうしたものかと悩みました。

そんな想いを抱いて、富山の岩瀬町を訪れたときに、今、店に飾ってある安田泰三さんのガラス細工に出会いました。

15kgを超える、非常に力強い作品です。安田さんにうかがったら、これだけの大きな作品は、これが最後だと。体力的にもう無理だとおっしゃったのです。

この作品を見て、これを新しい六本木ヒルズ店に飾りたいと思ったのです。よし、やろうと、安田さんの作品から力をもらいました。それで、全面リニューアルするなら、森田さんにお願いしようと決めていましたので、森田さんにも安田さんの作品を見てもらったのです。

森田　乾さんと富山に安田さんの、その

Toyama to see Yasuda-san's masterpiece.

**Inui** I relied on Morita-san for the designing so I didn't want to push him into using Yasuda-san's work. We went to see the work together and I told him how this artwork inspired me to go on with the renovation, and if it inspires him in any way, it would be great to see it displayed somewhere in the restaurant.

**Morita** After hearing that, there's no way I wouldn't integrate it into the designing, you know? I decided to place this artwork in the center and started designing from there. We can't forget that this is a *kushi-nobo* restaurant and that we need a hood over the burner. I decided to place the hood symmetrically, with a design to enhance this glass artwork. I then came up with the idea to place his other art-works all over the restaurant.

**Inui** I thought "wow this is a lot…"and to be honest the budget crossed my

大作を見に行きましたね。

乾　内装デザインは森田さんにお任せしたわけですから、「これを飾ってください」と口出しはしたくありませんでしたので、作品を実際に見てもらいながら、「この作品から力をもらって六本木ヒルズ店の改装を決めました。もしよかったら、新しい六本木店のどこかに飾ってください」と言ったのです。

森田　それ聞いたら、置かないわけにいきませんよね(笑)。むしろ、この作品を中心にデザインを考え、カウンター正面の真ん中に象徴として置いたのです。そして、串揚げ店ですから、揚げる鍋の上にフードが必要なのですが、そのフードも、この作品がきれいに見えるようにシンメトリーにして、この作品を浮き上がらせて見せるデザインにしました。さらに、客席のいろいろなところに安田さんの作品を置くことを提案しました。

乾　「え、こんなに安田さんの作品を置くの?」と思ったのと同時に、予算のことが思い浮かびましたね(笑)。率直に、安田さんに相談して、安田泰三美術館的

mind. Right away I talked with Yasuda-san and decided to create this space into a Yasuda Taizo Museum. I asked Yasuda-san to display 20 of his artworks in his liking and added information and commentary to each work.

### Worker-friendly design

**Inui** The space itself is actually larger than the previous Roppongi Hills venue, but I minimized the number of seats to allow comfortable and spacious seating. I also asked for a design where it's easier for the workers to move around. I believe a worker-friendly space is also guest-friendly.

**Morita** Inui-san is a design enthusiast so our meetings went quite smoothly. He comes up with many ideas that build up to what he wants to achieve. As a designer, I consider him a fun partner to work with. At the same time, I do feel the pressure to realize his requests, of course.

な空間にしました。店内に自由に安田さんの作品を置いてもらい、作品の解説書も用意して、20数個飾らせていただきました。

## 働きやすさも重視した設計

**乾** 前の六本木ヒルズ店より店は広くなりましたが、席数は減らしました。ゆったりとお食事をしていただけるのと、従業員の働く動線も意識して設計をお願いしました。従業員が働きやすいということは、お客様の居心地の良さにつながると思います。

　経営効率もデザインの中から生み出せるので、森田さんとは事前にかなり打ち合わせしましたね。

**森田** 乾さんはデザインが好きなので、打ち合わせをしやすいんです。いろいろなアイデアが出てきて、やりたいことが明確になってくるんです。デザイナーとして、一緒に仕事をして楽しいパートナーですね。その分、いろいろな要望をどうやって実現させようか、プレッシャーも大きくなって悩むのですがね(笑)。

## To express the profoundness of a historical restaurant

**Morita**  It's not everyday that I can work with a 70-year old restaurant. I wanted to keep that one-of-a-kind profound feeling so I decided to create the largest noren (curtain at the entrance) the guests have ever seen. I also revived the old Kushinobo logo. While I was designing this noren, I thought I wanted a nice piece of noren holder to go with it.

**Inui**  I couldn't believe my ears when Morita-san told me to ask Tsutomu Iwasaki to make a noren holder; Iwasaki-san is a world-renowned sculptor. I had been friends with Iwasaki-san but I knew he was extremely busy, so I asked him expecting him to say no. It turns out Iwasaki-san had been a fan of Morita-san's work, and that he would be happy to work with him.

**Morita**  It's a noren holder like no other, there's not a same one in the world. I

## 老舗の重厚感をアートで表現

**森田**　なかなか創業70年の飲食店は少ないですから、老舗感は大事にしたいと思い、見たこともないような大きな暖簾を作り、そこに昔の店のマークを復活させました。
この暖簾を作っていく中で、暖簾受けをいいのにしたいなあと思ったんです。

**乾**　「暖簾受け、岩﨑努さんに頼んでください」と森田さんに言われたときは、耳を疑いました(笑)岩﨑さんは、世界中からオファーが来る著名な彫刻家ですから。
　岩﨑さんとは知己の仲でしたが、超多忙な人でしたので、断られることを承知でお願いしました。そしたら、岩﨑さんが、「僕は森田さんのファンで、森田さんの仕事に関われるのなら、ぜひやらせてほしい」と言ってくれたのです。

**森田**　世界に一つだけの暖簾受けですね。炎をテーマに作っていただいて、お

asked for something along the theme of fire, and I believe this gave the restaurant its matching prestige.

The countertop and hood are decorated with white and gold Japanese urushi lacquer, a work by Yui Higashibata from Kyoto.

The box seating in front of the hood works like a theater seat, where the guests can see the chefs' cooking as a theater performance. It's one of the popular seats among our guests. The acrylic artwork with skewers is a piece by Tsuyoshi Yamamoto from Osaka. He said the number of skewers he used is 108 which matches the number of Kleshas in Buddhism, and I was so impressed. These artworks are placed not too elaborately, just like a museum, but not too formal, resulting in a very comfortable space.

**Inui** Another person to mention is Gaku Shakunaga, a ceramic artist. It has become a must for a known chef to have Shakunaga-san's dinnerware in their restaurants. Although we only had three months until the opening, he was kind enough to prepare his ceramic works for

店に箔が付きました。

　他にも、カウンタートップやフードのところの白とゴールドの装飾は、漆なのです。京都の東端唯さんの作品です。

　フードの前のボックス風の席は、そこから見ると職人さんが串を揚げている姿が舞台を見ているような、観客になったよう感じになれる席で、居心地がいいと言ってもらっています。

　アクリルの中に串揚げの串を入れたアクリルアートも飾りました。大阪の山本剛さんの作品で、でき上ってきたら、「108本入れました」って。煩悩の数って、やるなあと思いました(笑)。

　さりげなく、ところどころにアートワークがあって、ミュージアムのようで、でも、堅苦しくない空間になりました。

**乾**　もう一人、陶芸家が参加してくれています。釋永岳さんです。釋永さんの作品を置くというのが有名シェフのステイタスにもなっています。開店の1か月前に注文したのにもかかわらず、作っていただけました。

us.

The 7.30m countertop Masuda-san has provided us is also a piece of art.

**Morita**   The pictures displayed on the walls are my own works. They are of oil, panko bread crumbs, and rice flour; the must ingredients of *kushinobo*.

**Inui**   I wish that eating at Kushinobo will become something like a fashion statement. But that doesn't mean we hold a high threshold. Our Roppongi venue is family-friendly; we welcome infants as well.

We've been running Kushinobo for 70 years. There are guests who come with their grandchildren, telling them that they themselves used to come here when they were children.

**Morita**   I left a space right next to the noren at the entrance, and I'm glad I did so because I see that the guests are able to place their strollers there.

桝田酒造の桝田社長が用意してくれた7メートル30センチの檜の1枚板のカウンターも、ある意味、アートですね。

**森田**　僕も写真で参加させてもらいました。串揚げに使う、油、パン粉、米粉の写真を飾らせてもらっています。全体としては、何十年経っても古くならないデザインを追求しました。

**乾**　「『串の坊』で串揚げを食べることが何よりおしゃれ」と、言ってもらえるようになりたいなあと思っています。かといって敷居を高くするということはありません。『串の坊』は六本木ヒルズ店も幼児連れの方もオーケーです。

　70年営業していると、お孫さんを連れて来られて、「おじいちゃんも子供の頃にここによく来たんだよ」って孫に話しているお客様も多いのです。こういうお客様を大事にしていきたいのです。

**森田**　大暖簾の横が、ベビーカーの駐輪スペースになっていたりして、このスペース作っておいてよかったなあと思います(笑)。

**Inui**  Kushinobo traditions have come a long way, and I feel that I'm just merely riding on top of all the hardships by the people that built this place for years. The restaurant is renewed, but I feel obligated to pay respect to those who have worked in this restaurant by keeping its traditions. I am truly satisfied with the new Kushinobo Roppongi Hills.

**Morita**  I agree, it's a truly remarkable restaurant.

**Inui**  Thank you very much for your time today.

乾　『串の坊』の伝統は長く、いろいろな人が苦労して積み重ねてきた上に、自分は今のっかっていると思うのです。店は新しくしても、これまでがんばってきた人たちに失礼がないように守るところは守っていきたいのです。六本木ヒルズ店は、会心の店だと思います。

森田　ほんと、僕もいい店だと思います。

乾　本日は、ありがとうございました。

## 2006 Why is kushinobo So Enjoyable?
## 2006 串揚げは、なぜ楽しいか？

**Sato** Which sauce would you recommend for this beef *kushinobo*?

**Inui** You can use any type of sauce on *kushinobo*. Really, it can be anything you like, *kushinobo* sauce, ketchup, salt, or ponzu. It depends on what you are drinking with the meal, sake or shochu, and on your taste.

**Sato** I usually take a bite to see what it tastes like before deciding which sauce to use. Since I'm from Kansai, I must admit that I have a preconceived inclination to eat cabbage with *kushinobo* sauce.

**Nishi** In that case, I will eat it with salt. Yum, it is delicious.

佐藤　これは牛肉の串揚げですが、店としては何を付けて食べたらいいと提案されるのですか。

乾　僕は串揚げは何付けてもいいと思ってまして、ソースなのかケチャップなのか塩なのかポン酢なのかは各々のお好みでという考えですね。だって日本酒飲んだり焼酎飲んだり、串揚げと一緒に楽しむお酒によっても、何を付けたいかも変わるだろうし、もちろん好みもありますから。

佐藤　私はまず基本的に何も付けないで食べてみて、それで何を付けて食べたらいいかなと考えたいですね。ただ、私は関西人なので、ソースはキャベツに付けて食べるものかなという先入観はありますね。

西　では、僕は塩を付けていただきます。おいしいです。

**Chairman**
**Haruhiko Inui**
乾　晴彦

Kushinobo CO.,LTD.
President

株式会社串の坊
代表取締役社長

**Youichi Sato**
佐藤陽一

Wien dining MAXIVIN,
the main sommelier
Winner of Japan Sommelier
Contest 2005

ワインダイニング
「マクシヴァン」
オーナーソムリエ
2005年日本ソムリエ
コンクール優勝

**Ryuichiro Masuda**
桝田隆一郎

Masuda Sake Company LTD.
(Masuizumi Brewery)
President

株式会社桝田酒造店
「満寿泉」蔵元
代表取締役

**Youichiro Nishi**
西陽一郎

Nishi Sake Brewing CO.,LTD.
(Tominohouzan Brewery)
President

西酒造株式会社
「富乃宝山」蔵元
代表社員

**Sato** It even goes well with mustard.

**Masuda** *Kushinobo* is a fascinating dish because you can eat it with any type of sauce. It also goes well with different types of drinks.

**Inui** It seems that we have all come to a decision. I guess this meeting is over. (Laughter) *Kushinobo* is enjoyable because there is no particular topping you need to eat it with. Today you can have it with *Kushinobo* sauce, tomorrow you can eat it with salt. That's why you can eat at *kushinobo* as many times as you want and have a different meal each time.

### Which drink goes well with *kushinobo*?

**Masuda** I'm really enjoying this meal because we are supposed to discuss which *kushinobo* goes with which drink. Some restaurants sell sake by blind-tasting 3 different types. Since *kushinobo* goes well with sake, shochu, or wine, it might be a good idea to offer an assortment of drinks as one item on the menu.

**Nishi** We're having fun today because everyone here enjoys drinking.

**佐藤** マスタードも合いますよ。

**桝田** そういうふうに、食べ方に決まりがなくて何付けても楽しめるし、いろいろなお酒に合うのが串揚げの魅力なんですね。

**乾** もう、結論が出てしまいまして、これで座談会は終わってしまいますよ。(笑) 串揚げの楽しみ方は、この串揚げにはこれを付けるということを決めないことによって、今日はソースを付けたけど、次に来たときには塩で、という食べ方をすることなんです。だから『kushinobo』の料理は何回行っても同じ味にならないんです。

### 串揚げに合うお酒は何？

**桝田** 今日は座談会のテーマを意識して、どの串揚げとどのお酒を組み合わせるといいのかなと考えながら食べているわけですが、すごく楽しいですね。よく日本酒を3種類をセットにして利き酒してもらうような売り方はありますが、串揚げには日本酒も焼酎もワインも合うわけだから、いろいろなお酒とあらかじめセットにして提供されるのも楽しいですね。

**西** ここに居るみんな酒好きですから、特に楽しいですよ。

**Sato**  You don't know what the next dish is in *kushinobo*. Just looking at the dish, you may think that because it is asparagus, white wine will go well with it. After a bite you realize that it is wrapped in sliced pork and wonder whether red wine would have been better, but actually white wine is just as delicious.

**Nishi**  Shochu doesn't contain any extracts. That's why it goes well with any dish and doesn't interfere with the taste. There are no strict rules with shochu, as there are with wine. Lately, I enjoy drinking shochu on the rocks before going on to sake. I would definitely like to expand on this idea. I believe that *kushinobo* is the type of dish that offers an entertainment based on mix-and-match.

**Masuda**  Some connoisseurs say that you should drink only sake or only shochu with your meal, but I don't agree. They can be consumed together at the same meal.

**Nishi**  They are both Japanese drinks, so they can be enjoyed with various types of dishes.

佐藤　串揚げは次に何が出てくるかわからないですよね。しかも、見た目だけで判断して、たとえばアスパラだからと白ワインを飲んで、おいしいなあと。食べてから豚肉が巻いてあることを知って、じゃあ赤のほうだったかなというとそうでもなくて、白ワインもきちんと合ってくれる。

西　焼酎は材料のエキスが入ってない酒でしょ。だから、食べ合わせはなく、どんな食事も邪魔しないのが焼酎です。逆に、ワインのように、この料理にはこの焼酎という絶妙なマリアージュは焼酎にはないですね。ただ、最近思うのは、焼酎のロックを飲んで、次に清酒を飲む、そんな流れの楽しさですね。この楽しみ方が広がればいいなあと思います。こんな楽しみ方のできる料理が串揚げだと思います。

桝田　確かに、日本酒がいいか焼酎がいいか一方を選んで、一方だけで料理を楽しむのではなく、共存ですよね。

西　同じ「日本のお酒」だから、いろいろな料理と一緒に楽しむのが理屈抜きでいいでしょう。

**Sato** Green beans wrapped in sliced pork go well with wine, but since *kushinobo* is served hot, the flavor of meat stays in the mouth after it is eaten. The taste juices up and goes well with sake. With *kushinobo*, you can enjoy finding the right chemistry with a variety of drinks during your meal.

**Each skewer is a complete dish**

**Inui** Here I will describe some of the skewers. This is matsutake mushrooms. The citrus sudachi is a specialty from Tokushima. The squid skewer is a large cuttlefish with a raw, elegant sea urchin on top.

**Sato** *Kushinobo* is a type of deep fried dish in which the taste of the ingredients is particularly enjoyable.

**Nishi** You are quite right. Also, it isn't oily, even though we have eaten quite a number of skewers.

**Sato** The texture of the food plays a major role in enjoying *kushinobo*. It has a crispy feel. What is this dish with the bone?

佐藤　インゲンの豚肉巻きにはワインが合わせやすいのかと思うのですが、実際、串揚げは温かく、お肉の香りが食べてからも残るので、冷たい日本酒と楽しんでも違和感がなく生きてきます。食べてみて、新たにいろいろなお酒との相性が発見できるのが串揚げですね。

## 1本1本が、完成した料理

乾　料理の説明をします。これは松茸。スダチは徳島特産。イカは紋甲イカに生のバフンウニをのせています。

佐藤　串揚げは、揚げ物というジャンルの中の1つのスタイルだと思うのですが、今回は特に素材を味わっている、という感じもありますね。

西　本当にそうですね。それにこれだけ食べすんできても、油を感じない。

佐藤　串揚げの楽しみの中に「食感」というものが大きな位置を占めていますね。クリスピーなおいしさですね。この骨つきのは何ですか。

**Inui**  Chicken wings cut open, stuffed with minced shrimp, wrapped with seaweed and deep fried. We have served it at *kushinobo* for over 50 years. You can have it with either *kushinobo* sauce or salt. This skewer is parsley sandwiched in celery, and wrapped with bacon and kisu (a silvery fish). With each bite you get the flavor and texture of every ingredient.

**Sato**  Are the skewers served in a specific order?

**Inui**  No, there is no particular order. It varies with the chef and the customer. But we do try to serve a combination of meat, fish, and vegetables.

**Nishi**  Each skewer is like a small dish with its own little world of flavor. To be able to drink and to taste a variety of dishes one at a time is irresistible for people who enjoy drinking.

**Sato**  I agree. Every skewer is unique and original. Since they are deep fried, the initial feeling in the mouth is the same, but *kushinobo* transforms them into a potpourri of tastes. It could even be a striking texture or a flavor of curry.

**乾**  これは、鶏肉の手羽を開いて、海老ミンチを詰めて海苔で巻いて揚げたものです。これはもう50年以上前から『kushinobo』にある一品です。これも、ソースでも塩でもお好きなのもを付けて召し上がってください。これはセロリの間にパセリをはさんで、ベーコンを巻いて、さらにキスで巻いたものです。ひと口で食べると、それぞれの食感と風味が広がります。

**佐藤**  出す順番は決まっているのですか。

**乾**  順番は決めてません。作り手によっても順番は違うし、お客さまによってもまちまち。なんとなく肉と魚と野菜を混ぜながら出すようにはしています。

**西**  でも、一本一本が、小皿料理のようですね。それぞれに味の世界があるというか。いろいろな料理を少しずつ楽しみながらお酒が飲めるというのは、お酒の好きな人にはたまらないですよ。

**佐藤**  ほんと、一本一本が個性豊かです。揚げ物なので、口に入れる初めの温度は同じくらいですが、串揚げはその後の変化が多彩ですね。カレー風味が際立ったり、食感が楽しめたり。

**Masuda** Since I am a sake brewer, I would like to conclude this discussion by asserting that the best match for *kushinobo* is sake. (Laughter) But aside from this joke, I do really believe that *kushinobo* goes well with any drink.

**Inui** It is astonishing, isn't it?

**Masuda** There are no strict rules as to which drink goes well with *kushinobo*. And as Inui-san said, there are no strict rules as to which topping goes with which *kushinobo*. It can be *kushinobo* sauce or salt.

**Inui** That's the difference between *kushinobo* and kushikatsu from Osaka. The common kushikatsu sold in Osaka always uses a Worcestershire-based sauce. It is delicious; Osaka can be proud of it. But *kushinobo* emphasizes the ingredients and can be eaten with an assortment of sauces and drinks. Moreover, most of its ingredients are not unusual. Breadcrumbs and flour can be found anywhere in the world.

**Masuda** You're right. When Inui-san made *kushinobo* in Africa, he used toothpicks instead of skewers and fish from Lake Victoria. The fish was exquisite when made into *kushinobo*.

**桝田** 私は日本酒を作っているので、串揚げには日本酒が合う、という結論に持っていきたいんだけれど（笑）、本当にどのお酒にも串揚げはよく合います。

**乾** それは不思議といえば不思議ですよね。

**桝田** この串揚げにはソースで、この串揚げには塩、ということが決められないと乾さんは最初におっしゃったけど、お酒も同じではないですか。この串揚げにはこのお酒という厳密な相性はきめられないですね。

**乾** そこが大阪の串カツと『kushinobo』の違いでもあるんです。大阪の大衆的な串カツはソースしかないです。それはそれで大変おいしくて、大阪が誇れる食文化です。『kushinobo』の串揚げは素材の味わいを大切にし、お酒もいろいろな種類のものと楽しめるのが特徴ですね。かといって、材料は特別なものはない。パン粉も小麦粉も世界中にある。

**桝田** そう。この前、乾さんにアフリカで串揚げ食べさせてもらったんです。串の代わりに楊枝を使って。ビクトリア湖で釣った魚で。臭いのある魚だったけれど、串揚げにするとおいしかったです。

Inui  I believe that *kushinobo* will become more popular than tempura throughout the world.

Masuda  Today I'm eating most of my *kushinobo* without any *kushinobo* sauce.

Inui  That's it! When you're drinking beer, champagne, wine, sake, or shochu while you eat *kushinobo*, *kushinobo* sauce is sometimes so pungent that it drowns out the flavour of the beverage.

Sato  Try wrapping cabbage and eat it with a lot of *kushinobo* sauce. That's the way we eat it back home in Osaka. (Laughter)

### A dish that inspires the sake brewer!?

Masuda  Probably *kushinobo* (unlike sashimi) will go well with warmed sake that has cooled down. And *kushinobo* is good with sake on the rocks. When sake made from pure rice is taken out of the refrigerator and left on the table for some time, usually the temperature of the sake rises and no longer goes well with the food.  But somehow it isn't a problem with hot *kushinobo* that is served one after another.

乾　天ぷらより串揚げのほうがより世界中にウケると思いますよ。

桝田　でも、今日はあんまりソースを使って食べてないなあ。

乾　そうなんです。串揚げをビールとだけでなく、シャンパンやワインや日本酒や焼酎と一緒にきちんと味わって食べようとすると、ソースの存在が薄れてくるんです。ソースはインパクト強いですから、別の串揚げでもソースを付けると同じ味に感じやすいんです。

佐藤　キャベツをぐるぐると巻いて、ソースにひたして食べてください。これが大阪生まれの私のこだわりです。（笑）

### 蔵元を刺激する料理！？

桝田　この純米酒は、冷蔵庫から出してテーブルの上に置かれてずいぶん時間が経ってます。温度が上がって料理に合わなくなってくるものですが、温かい串揚げを次々出されると合うんですよ。たぶん、燗冷ましでも合うんですよ。ロックでも合うんですよ。日本酒をおいしく飲ませる料理としてはピッタリですね。お刺し身を食べながらぬるい日本酒になると合わなくなるとかあるんです。

**Sato**  Wouldn't the brewers be appalled seeing ice in their sake?

**Masuda**  On the contrary, new ideas and curiosities are worth exploring, such as adding Perrier, making sake with more acidity that will go with this *kushinobo*, or even making sparkling sake with an acid taste.

**Sato**  I thought that the sake brewers would be appalled if we drank sake with ice. Can I try this with ice? And I hope you don't mind if I shake the bottle. It should make the sake mellower.

**Nishi**  Shaking a bottle of shochu also makes it easier to drink. We should look for different ways of drinking sake.

**Inui**  Is it really all right to put ice into sake?

**Masuda**  Adding warm water or adding ice to sake is an orthodox drink. You shouldn't add fruit juice, though.

佐藤　氷を日本酒に浮かべても作り手として怒らないんですか？

桝田　怒らないし、ペリエを入れて飲んでみたらどうかとか、この串揚げに合わせてもう少し酸味のある日本酒を作ってみたいとか。発泡性で酸味のある日本酒を作ってみたいとか、串揚げを食べていると好奇心が湧きますね。

佐藤　日本酒は氷を入れて飲んだら蔵元の人に怒られる、というイメージがありましたよ。じゃあ、さっそく氷入れて飲んでみていいですか。ついでにといっては何ですが、瓶も振らせてもらいます。飲みやすくなるはずです。

西　焼酎も振ると飲みやすくなりますよ。日本酒はこれまで素材ばかりにこだわり過ぎてきたから。飲み方をもっと提案するといいですよね。

乾　本当にいいんですか？　日本酒に氷を入れて提供しても。

桝田　日本酒をお湯で割るとか、氷を入れるのは正統派です。果汁を入れてとかになると話は別ですが。

Sato  You can tell your customers that the sake we have chosen won't change its taste even if it is on the rocks. This is one kind of service they will appreciate.

Nishi  When the ice melts and the alcohol content of the sake drops, it awakens the sweetness of the rice and the taste can be reevaluated when the taste of alcohol disappears.

Inui  It's interesting to see a shochu brewer orate on sake.

Nishi  Sorry about that.  (Laughter) I've always said that because sake and shochu are both drinks born in Japan, we should work together instead of competing with each other.

Masuda  You're right. Shochu is delicious as well. I should be lauding shochu like this as a sake brewer.

Inui  It is grand to have sake and shochu brewers get together at *kushinobo*, eating platefuls of the world-renowned *kushinobo*, and expanding their imagination into new ways of producing sake and shochu. This is a great way to conclude a book on *kushinobo*. (Laughter) I had a great time today, thanks to you all. Good *kushinobo* depends not only on the beverages but on the type of company one keeps.

佐藤　氷を入れても本来の個性を失わない日本酒を選んでいるのでロックで飲んで頂いてもいいですよ、というサービスする側からのお客さまへの提案も大切でしょうね。

西　氷が少し溶けて、日本酒のアルコール度数が下がると、あるところからアルコールを感じなくて、米の甘さがまた引き立ってきて、おいしさを再認識できるんですよ。

乾　焼酎の蔵元として、そんなに熱く日本酒のこと語っていいんですか。

西　いやあ（笑）。僕は日本酒も焼酎も日本の酒だからって言い続けているんです。お互い足を引っ張るんじゃなくて、切磋琢磨です。

桝田　いやいや、焼酎もおいしいですよ。こういう風に日本酒の蔵元として焼酎も褒めてかないとだめですね。

乾　日本酒の蔵元のかたも、焼酎の蔵元のかたも『kushinobo』に来て、世界に通用する串揚げをたくさん食べていただいて、その上で新しい日本酒と新しい焼酎づくりのイマジネーションを広げてもらうのがいいですね。串揚げの本らしい、まとめになりました（笑）。皆さん、今日は楽しかったです。おいしい串揚げを楽しむのに大切なのは、お酒ももちろん、メンバーですね。

## 2019 Why is kushinobo so enjoyable?
## 2019 串揚げは、なぜ楽しいか？

**Inui**  Once again, thank you for gathering here today to discuss why *kushinobo* is so entertaining.

**Nishi**  So this is a continuation from page 156 ,the last gathering. When was that?

**Inui**  It was back in 2005, so 14 years has passed.

**Masuda**  We were all so young!

**Inui**  I've been seeing all of you individually, but all four of us in one place like this has not happened since our last gathering.

**Sato**  Maybe because we have been seeing each other individually, it doesn't seem like that much time has passed. Our theme once again is the marriage of *kushinobo* and beverages. Wouldn't our conversation be the same?

**Inui**  The kushinobo we're serving today is from Kushinobo Special. It's an event we started in 2012, a course menu of *kushinobo* that you don't eat with sauce. Please enjoy each dish and let me hear your opinions on what drinks would match them.

**Masuda**  *Kushinobo* without sauce?

乾  また、前回同様に、「串揚げは、なぜ楽しいか？」を語っていただきたくためにお集まりいただきました。ありがとうございます。

西  前回って、156 ページの続きの座談会なんですか。あれ、何年前ですか。

乾  2005 年ですから、14 年前ですね。

桝田  みんな若いですねぇ（笑）。

乾  個別には、ちょくちょく会ってますが、この 4 人揃うのは、156 ページのときの座談会以来ですね。

佐藤  そう言われれば、そうですが、個別に会っているせいか、そんなに年数が経った感じがしませんね。でも、また、串揚げとお酒のマリアージュのテーマですが、おんなじ展開になりませんか？

乾  今日、お出しする串揚げは、串の坊 Special なんです。2012 年から始めた、ソースで食べない串揚げのコースの品なのです。それぞれ味わっていただきながら、どんなお酒と合うかを皆さんに語っていただきたいのです。

桝田  ソースで食べない串揚げがあるんですか。

**Chairman
Haruhiko Inui
乾　晴彦**

Kushinobo CO.,LTD.
President

株式会社串の坊
代表取締役社長

**Ryuichiro Masuda
桝田隆一郎**

Masuda Sake Company LTD.
(Masuizumi Brewery)
President

株式会社桝田酒造店
「満寿泉」蔵元
代表取締役

**Inui** Yes. Let's get started, shall we? To start off, we have "Peony Shrimp, Sea Urchin, Egg, Caviar & Avocado".

**Masuda** This is a *kushinobo*?

**Inui** Yes. Avocado is fried and then wrapped with seaweed, stuffed with egg, peony shrimp, and sea urchin, with caviar on top. One bite will give you a quintet of flavors. It's an homage to a dish I had in Waku Ghin in Singapore, run by Tetsuya Wakuda.

**Sato** This goes well with a champagne. Usually the fish smell is left behind when raw fish and champagne are taken together, but that doesn't happen here. Maybe because it's fried, or because the champagne is good?

**Inui** Hopefully for both of those reasons. This champagne is HENRI GIRAUD. Next we have "240 Million Eyes". We fried a soft-boiled quail egg and topped it with caviar.

**Masuda** From Hiromi Go? (Note:"240 Million Eyes"is a famous song by Japanese singer Hiromi Go).

**Inui** For the story behind it, please see page24.

乾　まあ、お楽しみください。まずは、「牡丹海老、雲丹、卵、キャビア＆アボカド」の串揚げです。

桝田　これ、串揚げなんですか。

乾　そうです。アボカドを揚げて海苔で巻き、中には卵、牡丹海老、雲丹を詰め込み、その上にキャビアをのせました。ひと口で食べると、味の五重奏に魅了されます。シンガポールのWAKUGIN（和久田哲也さんの店）で食べた料理に感動して、それをオマージュした串揚げです。

佐藤　これ、シャンパーニュに合いますね。生の魚とシャンパンを合わせると、生臭さが残ることが多いんですが、残りませんね。串揚げだからなのか、シャンパーニュがおいしいからでしょうか。

乾　両方でしょうね（笑）。シャンパーニュは、アンリージローです。次は「二億四千万の瞳」です。ウズラの半熟卵を串揚げにして、その上にキャビアをのせました。

桝田　Hiromi Go ですか。

乾　くわしい開発話は、24 ページを見

***Youichi Sato***
佐藤陽一

Wien dining MAXIVIN,
the main sommelier
Winner of Japan Sommelier
Contest 2005

ワインダイニング
「マクシヴァン」
オーナーソムリエ
2005 年日本ソムリエ
コンクール優勝

***Youichiro Nishi***
西陽一郎

Nishi Sake Brewing CO.,LTD.
(Tominohouzan Brewery)
President

西酒造株式会社
「富乃宝山」蔵元
代表社員

**Nishi** This also matches well with champagne, but it also goes well with shochu and sake. The tastes don't fight each other.

**Sato** You can enjoy it more when you place the caviar directly on your tongue.

## Enjoying a variety of drinks

**Inui** Next we have "Sweet & Sour Pork". This is Hozan Pork, which was raised with potatoes that were used in making shochu at Nishi-san's brewery. Every year we think of new *kushinobo* ideas using this pork.

**Sato** This literally is "Sweet & Sour Pork". With black pepper, this will go well with red wine.

**Nishi** Each menu makes me want to try it with different drinks.

**Masuda** Just like we have a sake variety set in some restaurants where we can try different kinds of sake, maybe Kushinobo can try a similar set with sake and red wine and let our guests enjoy each dish

てください（笑）。

**西** これも、シャンパーニュともちろん合いますが、焼酎がいいし、日本酒ともいいですね。味わいがケンカしないというか。

**佐藤** トッピングのキャビアを舌の上にのせるように食べると、おいしい串揚げですね。

## 次々と、いろいろなお酒が飲みたくなる

**乾** 次は「黒豚酢豚」です。こちらの西さん蔵の焼酎を蒸留した後の芋で育てた黒豚です。とてもおいしくて、その宝山豚を使った串揚げを毎年考えています。

**佐藤** 酢豚がソースというわけですね。これ、黒胡椒をふると、赤ワインに合うと思います。

**西** それぞれ、いろいろなお酒と楽しみたくなりますね。

**桝田** 利き酒セットといって、日本酒を飲み比べるセットがありますが、串揚げには、日本酒と焼酎と赤ワインをセット

with different drinks. That could be an idea.

**Inui**  Next we have "Pickled Tuna and Konowata (salted entrails of sea cucumber)", with shari (fried sushi rice). The pickled tuna is an homage to Komatsu Yasuke in Kanazawa, who also gave me this konowata.

**Sato**  Shall we try Masuda-san's sake "8888", a Masuizumi made in Chivas Regal Barrel? Why did you name it "8888"?

**Masuda**  It turns out that the distance between Chivas Regal in Scotland and our brewery is exactly 8,888 kilometers.

**Sato**  That's a very interesting trivia. Masuizumi is barreled and revived in a very good way.

**Nishi**  Some people say sushi ingredients and champagne don't match, but that doesn't seem to be the case here.

**Sato**  Sushi and champagne is a nice match, actually. From a sommelier's point of view, it's not best if you drink champagne while there's sushi left in your

にして、串揚げごとに合わせながら楽しんでください、というのもいいですね。

**乾**  次は、「鮪漬け、海鼠腸」です。シャリが揚がっています。漬けは金沢の小松弥助のオマージュです。海鼠腸は小松弥助さんから譲っていただいたものです。

**佐藤**  シーバースリーガルの樽に桝田さんのところの「満寿泉」を漬けた「8888」を合わせて見ますか。その前にどうして「8888」なんですか。

**桝田**  うちの蔵とスコットランドのシーバースリーガルの蒸留所との距離が偶然にも丁度8888キロメートルなのです。

**佐藤**  へぇ。樽詰めと言っても、満寿泉を生かした仕上がりになっている感じで、いい意味で面白いお酒ですね。

**西**  寿司ネタとシャンパーニュは合わないという人がいますが、これも合いますね。

**佐藤**  寿司とシャンパーニュは合いますよ。ソムリエ的に言うと、寿司を食べて、まだ、口の中に残っている状態でシャンパーニュを飲むと合わないのです。寿司

mouth. Eat sushi, swallow it with your saliva, and then drink champagne.

**Nishi** But a sweeter champagne wouldn't work well because its sugar content fights with that of sushi.

**Inui** Next up is "Herring Roe on Kelp, and Ezo Bafun Sea Urchin". Herring roe on kelp is our classic here at Kushinobo, and we decided to top it with plenty of raw sea urchin. A very luxurious *kushinobo*, for sure.

**Nishi** The herring roe and sea urchin both have very rich smell that match hot sake.

**Inui** Next, we have the main dish of the day. A soft fugu roe *kushinobo* topped with white truffle.

**Masuda** This goes with sake. Sake has so much variety of taste and it's very entertaining to match each *kushinobo* with different sake.

**Sato** Hot sake is great but to be precise,

を食べて、唾液を飲み込んでからシャンパーニュを飲むと、すごく合うのです。

**西** シャンパーニュでも、甘口は寿司と糖の種類が違うのでケンカして合わないですけどね。

**乾** 次は「子持ち昆布、馬糞雲丹」です。『串の坊』の昔からの定番の子持ち昆布の串揚げに生雲丹をたっぷりのせました。これも超高級串揚げです。

**西** 子持ち昆布と馬糞雲丹は、香りが豊かですね。この香味は熱燗にあいますね。

**乾** 次は、本日のメインディッシュとも言える「ふぐの白子」の串揚げ、白トリュフのトッピングです。

**桝田** これも日本酒がいいですね。やはり、日本酒は味わいが多彩で、いろいろな日本酒を串揚げに合わせて楽しむのはいいですね。

**佐藤** 熱燗もいいですが、20℃くらいに

sake at around 20°C would create the best synergy.

## Layering flavors

**Inui** Next, we have "Squid, Sea Urchin, Beach Silvertop, and Sesame with shari (fried sushi rice)".

**Masuda** Is this squid filleted into three pieces?

**Inui** Of course, it's Komatsu Yasuke's squid. This too is an homage dish to Komatsu Yasuke.

**Sato** This kushinobo is on a whole another level. Shouldn't you rename it?

**Nishi** Wow, this is a genre called Kushinobo.

**Inui** It still is a simple fried skewer, and because I want keep upgrading this category, I'd rather keep its name. I wish for people to think it is a simple fried skewer, but Kushinobo serves the best one.

**Sato** The difference between *kushinobo* and tempura is that you can layer the flavors. By layering and adding on the ingredients, the complexity of flavours adds up

上げた日本酒が、この串揚げと引き立て合うと思います。

## 味を重ねられるのも、串揚げの魅力

**乾** 次は「剣先烏賊、雲丹、浜防風、胡麻」でシャリが揚がっています。

**桝田** この烏賊、三枚におろしてますか。

**乾** 小松弥助さんの烏賊ですから。これも小松弥助さんの定番料理のオマージュです。

**佐藤** 従来の串揚げと別格ですね。別の名称にしたほうがいいのではないですか。

**西** そお、ほんと、kushinobo という料理ですよ。

**乾** たかが串カツですが、それをレベルアップして行きたいので、別の名称にはしたくないんです。串揚げだけれど、串の坊が最高級だ、というのを目指したいのです。どうでしたか、今日の串の坊 Special は。

**佐藤** 串揚げは、天ぷらと違って、いろいろと味を重ねることができることがわ

and enlarges the possibilities to match with different types of drinks.

**Nishi** This *kushinobo* is filled with love. It's the kind of love that let you enjoy your drinks. I had no idea that there are so many *kushinobos* that can be enjoyed without any sauce.

**Masuda** The taste changes from one to the other and it makes you keep guessing what's coming next. Good taste is a minimum factor here. I do believe *kushinobo* is a dish that make people happy. I truly felt that today because I was able to enjoy good food and good drinks with good company.

**Inui** Yes, that is true. But my wish is for our restaurant Kushinobo to provide *kushinobo* that is always enjoyable no matter who you eat it with. Thank you very much for your time today, see you again in 14 years and let's talk about *kushinobo* once again.

かりました。味を重ねることで、味の複雑味が増すので、合わせられるお酒に広がりも出ます。

**西** この串揚げには、愛がありますね。お酒をおいしく味わえるようにする愛もあります。ソースで食べない串揚げが、こんなにあるとは驚きました。

**桝田** ひとつ一つ味が変わって、次は何が出てくるのだろうと、ワクワクの連続です。おいしいのは当たり前で、串揚げは人を幸せにする料理だなあと思いました。今日は、楽しい仲間と飲んで食べたから、よけいにそう感じました（笑）。

**乾** もちろんそうですけど、『串の坊』の串揚げは誰と食べても楽しい、というようにしたいんですよね。今日は、ありがとうございます。では、また、14年後、みんなで集まって串揚げの座談会をしましょう（笑）。

# Kushinobo is fantastic!

***Tatsuo Kamon***
嘉門タツオ

Comedian/singer/songwriter

## Let's globalize Kushinobo!
## 世界にはばたけ！日本の串揚げ！

It goes without saying that food that makes you feel good is always good. Among the wide variety of foods, kushikatsu — or rather, kushiage by *kushinobo* — tops the class in offering satisfaction.

Kushikatsu was originally an Osaka dish for men after work, in which ingredients covered with batter were deep-fried in unrefined oil. It was heavy on the stomach and gave heartburn if overeaten.

Although *kushinobo* is also a dish for the common people, it is a great improvement over kushikatsu. A sensitive new breath of air, it has mutated and evolved. It has perfected the uncouth kushikatsu and transformed it into a kushiage, with more depth of flavor.

Each bite-size piece is a microcosm of a dinner course, a contrast to those before and after. The repertoire of over 100 recipes

楽しい気分にさせてくれる食べる物は文句無くオイシイ。いろんな食べ物があるが「楽しさ」という点において「串カツ」は、いや「串の坊の串揚げ」はトップクラスだ。

元々「串カツ」とは、大阪で生まれたおおよそ雑多な「コロモをつけて、少々悪い油で揚げて、食べ過ぎると胸焼けなどをもよおす、ヘビーなオヤジの食べ物」だった。

庶民の食べ物である、という点に変わりはないが「串の坊」が「串カツ」を著しく発展させ、進化させたという事に間違いはない。近年その完成度は益々上昇し、雑多だったはずの「串カツ」に、より繊細な息吹が吹き込まれ「串揚げ」と名を変え、その奥行きが広がった。

パクッと一口で完結するわかりやすさがイイ。100種類以上あると言われるそれぞれの「小宇宙」は、食べる者に様々なイマジネーションを引き起こさせる。一体中身

excites the imagination of those who enjoy good food.

A delicious kushiage is concocted the moment it enters your mouth and you take that first bite. This is when you appreciate the enormous time taken to prepare and deep fry it. "I wonder what is inside and what combination of ingredients could create this flavor? Should I eat it with *kushinobo* sauce or with salt? Or should it be with ponzu sauce?" It's delightful to be able to improvise the taste.

It must be eaten hot! The real taste of kushiage can only be experienced when it is just out of the fryer!

Among all the deep-fried cuisines in the world, many have the attraction of being outstanding. But my aspiration lies in having all the people in the world try this delicate and enjoyable Japanese kushiage from *kushinobo*.

はどのような構成になっているのだろうか？どのような組み合わせでこの味が生まれるのか？

ソースをつけようか？塩にしようか？ポン酢にしようか？などと自分で采配出来るのも楽しい。

その「パクッ」と客の口に到達する一瞬までに、膨大な手間をかけ仕込み、揚げる瞬発力がうまく働いた時にのみ「ウマい串揚げ」が生まれる。

熱いうちに食べるべし！揚げたてこそ「串揚げ」の醍醐味。

世界に数多くの「揚げ物食文化」が存在する中、ダイナミックさが魅力という場合もある。しかし僕は「串の坊の串揚げ」のような、日本的でデリケートかつ文句なく楽しい「食べ物」を、世界中の人々に味わってもらいたい！

special thanks

| cooking | 調理 |
| --- | --- |
| Haruhiko Inui | 乾 晴彦 |
| Kouji Takahashi | 髙橋晃二 |
| Naokazu Moritomi | 守富直一 |
| Masahiro Chiba | 千葉真大 |
| Takeshi Yamazaki | 山崎威志 |

| transration adovisor | 英訳アドバイス |
| --- | --- |
| Robert Stanton | ロバート スタントン |
| Masahiro Inui | 乾 昌弘 |
| Aya Tanioka | 谷岡 彩 |

| sake | 日本酒 |
| --- | --- |
| Ryuichiro Masuda | 桝田隆一郎 |

| shou-chu | 焼酎 |
| --- | --- |
| Youichiro Nishi | 西陽一郎 |

| sommelier | ソムリエ |
| --- | --- |
| Youichi Sato | 佐藤陽一 |

| beverages | ビバレッジ |
| --- | --- |
| Satoshi Kimijima | 君嶋哲至 |

| design | デザイン |
| --- | --- |
| Yasumichi Morita | 森田 恭通 |

| graphic | グラフィック |
| --- | --- |
| Nakaba Kowzu | 高津 央 |

| china | 磁器 |
| --- | --- |
| Hideyuki Matsuzaki | 松崎英之 |

| cheese | チーズ |
| --- | --- |
| Zensaku Yoshida | 吉田全作 |

| photo in Sri Lanka | |
| --- | --- |
| Nobuyuki Aoki | 青木信之 |

| photo in Kenya | |
| --- | --- |
| Chikako Kurokawa | 黒川周子 |

Kushinobo Ltd.,Co.
3-5-20 Nakameguro Meguro-ku,Tokyo 153-0061
Tel. 03-3714-0094
http://www.kushinobo.co.jp

| cover photo | |
| --- | --- |
| Hiroyuki Goto | 後藤弘行（旭屋出版） |

| editor | |
| --- | --- |
| Hisanao Inoue | 井上久尚 |

| designer | |
| --- | --- |
| Yukio Tomikawa | 冨川幸雄 |

# kushinobo
### 串揚げとふぐ料理の新世界

2019年9月23日初版発行

| 著者 | Haruhiko Inui 乾 晴彦 |
| --- | --- |
| 発行者 | 早嶋 健 |
| 制作者 | 永瀬正人 |
| 発行所 | 株式会社旭屋出版 |

〒160-0005 東京都新宿区愛住町23-2
ベルックス新宿ビルⅡ 6階
Tel. 03-5369-6423（販売部）
Tel. 03-5369-6424（編集部）
Fax.03-5369-6431（販 売）

旭屋出版ホームページ　http://www.asahiya-jp.com

郵便振替00150-1-19572

印刷・製本　凸版印刷株式会社

ISBN4-7511-1369-1 C2077